DEVELOPING
COACHING
SKILLS

"*Developing Coaching Skills is an outstanding introduction to a wide range of coaching tools and methodologies. Whether you're a leader seeking to adopt a coaching approach to management, an aspiring coach establishing your practice, or an experienced coach looking to refresh your toolkit, you'll find this accessible volume a tremendously useful resource.*"

Ed Batista, Executive Coach, San Francisco (California)

"*An easily accessible and comprehensive book for the early career coach or student of coaching, full of useful exercises, the key models and approaches. A great place to start if you want to know what coaching is and how it works.*"

Dr Alexandra Morgan, Accredited Executive Coach and Programme Leader of the Postgraduate Certificate in Professional Coaching, Leicester Castle Business School (De Montfort University)

"*An insightful 'hands-on' coaching textbook, offering a concise and useful overview of coaching for those wishing to learn while practicing the fundamentals of coaching skills.*"

Dr Lorenzo Todorow, Executive Coach and Lecturer in Organisational Behaviour (UCL MBA), UCL School of Management (University College London)

"*If you want to develop your coaching skills, this is the book for you, it is practically a masterclass in your library! The integration of the 'what, why and how' is masterfully done with practical examples and insight from experienced global coaches. I am recommending this book because there isn't another on the market that captures the balance between theory and practice in this way!*"

Elona Hlatshwayo, Lecturer in Masters in Management in Business and Executive Coaching as a Lead for the Coaching Process and Professional Practice modules, Wits Business School, University of the Witwatersrand

"*Developing Coaching Skills provides a comprehensive, up-to-date guide for coaches and coach educators. It contains accessible exercises and case studies that bring skills development to life.*"

Dr Amy Stabler, Senior Lecturer, Leadership Development and Organisation Futures, Newcastle University Business School

DEVELOPING COACHING SKILLS

A Concise Introduction

DIETMAR STERNAD

econcise

Concise books for smart learners

Paperback ISBN: 978-3-903386-00-6
ePub ISBN: 978-3-903386-01-3
Kindle ISBN: 978-3-903386-02-0

Copy editor: Harriet Power
Cover design: Ajibola Akanji (creative_artz on fiverr)
Cover image by Stmool used under licence from Shutterstock.com

First published 2021 by **econcise publishing**
© 2021 econcise GmbH
Am Sonnengrund 14
A-9062 Moosburg (Austria)

www.econcise.com

CONTENTS

4 ESSENTIAL COACHING SKILLS

5 COACHING TOOLS

INTRODUCTION

Welcome to *Developing Coaching Skills: A Concise Introduction*!
Are you studying to **become a professional coach**? Do you want to enhance your coaching skills to become **a better coach or leader**? Or do you want to know more about how coaching works to help **improve the lives of others?**

Then this is the right book for you!

Coaching is now widely recognized as a **very effective method for helping other people to develop and succeed in their jobs and lives.** With this concise textbook, you will quickly gain a good overview of the principles of coaching. It will introduce you to key findings from coaching research, as well as the main methods and tools that coaches use in their daily practice.

Throughout the book, you will find **over 200 powerful coaching questions** that you can apply right away, several exercises for developing your own coaching skills, and in-depth insights into what experienced coaches do.

Thus, in a short time, you will gain a solid foundational knowledge of how coaching works.

At the same time, you can also use this book as a **practical guide for developing your own coaching skills.**

You may use these skills for becoming a better manager or team leader, for assisting your colleagues and friends when they are faced with challenging situations, or to prepare yourself for offering professional coaching services to other people and organizations.

Although we will focus on **coaching in the workplace**, you will also be able to use many of the approaches that are presented in this book in other contexts, such as when one of your friends or family members needs support in thinking through difficult issues.

Here is a short overview of **what you will learn** in the five chapters of this book:

- After reading **Chapter 1** (*What is coaching?*), you will know what coaching is all about, how it differs from other developmental activities, what effects and outcomes it has, what professional coaches do, and what it takes for coaching to be effective.
- In **Chapter 2** (*Effective coaching conversations*), you will learn how to conduct an effective coaching conversation in a goal- and solution-oriented way with the help of some of the most widely used coaching frameworks. Many powerful coaching questions are also included in this chapter.
- In **Chapter 3** (*The coaching process*), you will gain an overview of what professional coaches do during all the phases of a coaching process (including, for example, relationship-building with the coachee and the client organization, conducting coaching sessions and progress reviews, and a process evaluation).
- **Chapter 4** (*Essential coaching skills*) will help you to learn some of the most important coaching skills, including questioning, active listening, summarizing, and giving constructive feedback. It also contains information about how coaches and coachees can deal with difficult emotional situations.
- Finally, **Chapter 5** (*Coaching tools*) introduces a range of useful tools for coaches, including tools for raising a coachee's self-awareness, goal-setting tools, tools for reframing a problem, and tools for supporting the behavior change of coachees.

Taken together, the five chapters of this concise textbook will provide you with a compact yet comprehensive overview of the science and art of coaching.

Above all, it will help you to **acquire the skills that will enable you to effectively coach other people.**

"Talking with you really helped me to resolve this issue!"

"Thank you for the highly useful conversation—now I know what I will do about it tomorrow!"

"Thanks to your invaluable support, I was able to succeed!"

It can be very rewarding to get feedback like that and see other people grow and thrive as a consequence of your coaching conversations with them.

I hope that when you are developing your own coaching skills with the help of this book, you will have a lot of rewarding experiences like this, too!

SMARTER LEARNING

ACCESS FREE BONUS LEARNING MATERIALS

Learn smarter with our free additional learning resources that accompany *Developing Coaching Skills: A Concise Introduction*!

Both learners and lecturers can access the following additional learning materials in the 'Smart Learning' section on the book's companion website at www.econcise.com/coaching:

- **Mindmaps** that provide a succinct, visual 'big picture' overview of the key concepts in each chapter.
- **Links to videos** related to selected topics in the book.
- **Interactive flashcards** for a quick revision of the key concepts in each chapter.

If you are a lecturer, send us an email to lecturerservice@econcise.com. We can then provide you with editable **Microsoft PowerPoint® slides** for each chapter of this book and a set of **multiple-choice questions** for your exams.

If you want to stay informed about current developments in the field and get more information about new books for smart learners, you are also welcome to visit www.econcise.com/newsletter and subscribe to our newsletter!

WHAT IS COACHING?

....

This chapter will enable you to

- » Explain what coaching is all about.
- » Distinguish coaching from other types of developmental activities.
- » Describe the main outcomes of coaching.
- » Explore what professional coaches do.
- » Recognize the main factors that influence the effectiveness of coaching.

....

"Everyone needs a coach," said Bill Gates in a widely viewed TED Talk. "We all need people who give us feedback," he further explained. "That's how we improve."[1]

Helping others improve—whether at work or in their private life—lies at the core of what coaching is all about.

Working with a coach can help people increase their awareness of their own strengths and goals. It can help them take responsibility for their own development. It can enable them to determine what steps they need to take to achieve their goals.

In a relationship with a coach, people can also build specific skills, become more self-confident, improve their productivity and personal relationships, and grow through deep learning experiences. As a consequence, they can become more satisfied in their job or private life.

But how does it all work? Let us explore what coaches do to make such a positive impact on other people's lives.

What we mean when we talk about coaching

The English noun *coach* originally referred to a horse-drawn carriage (stemming from the Hungarian *kocsi [szekér]*, which means 'wagon from *Kocs*,' a small municipality in Hungary where coaches were manufactured). For a long time, the carriage was one of the most common means of transport that enabled people to travel from one place to another.

Similarly, coaching can be seen as a journey in which **a coach helps another person to travel from where they are now to where they would like to be in the future.**[2]

In this book, we use the following **definition of coaching**:

Coaching is a purposeful interaction in which one person (the coach) uses a questioning approach to help another person (the coachee) think through challenging issues, raise their self-awareness, consider their options, and take the right actions to realize their full potential and reach their personal or professional goals.

Let us take a closer look at the main elements of this definition:

- **Interaction**. The word *interaction* indicates that both the person who is coaching (the coach) and the person who is being coached (the coachee) play an important and active role in the process. The most typical form of coaching interaction is a conversation (or a series of conversations) between the coach and the coachee.
- **The coach**. The coach is the person who assists the coachee in thinking through challenging issues. In an organizational context, it can be a direct manager who uses a single coaching conversation to help one of their team members tackle a particular challenge. It can be a colleague or a friend who uses a coaching approach to support the coachee in determining the best action in a tricky situation. Or it can be a professional coach who serves the coachee as a longer-term sparring partner in a series of formal coaching sessions.
- **The purpose of coaching**. In a work context, coaching has the purpose of helping the coachee to become more effective in their job. Life coaches support their coachees in finding the right direction and reaching their goals in other areas of life beyond work. In either case, like a horse-drawn carriage, a coach enables the coachee to *reach a new place—*

whether in terms of learning new skills, gaining new insights about themselves or a particular situation, or setting and reaching new goals.

- **The questioning approach.** Intelligent questions are the main tools of a coach. Rather than giving advice to the coachee about what they should do, a good coach asks the right questions. Good coaching questions help the coachee to gain a better understanding of a situation and their own role in it. They also stimulate goal-oriented thinking and behavior. The questioning approach that experienced coaches follow has also become known as the *Socratic method*—named after the classical Greek philosopher Socrates, who used clever questioning to stimulate critical thinking in his discussions with other Athenians.

- **Realizing a coachee's full potential and helping them reach their goals.** Every world-class athlete has a coach who supports them in maximizing their full potential. Life coaches and, in a work context, executive coaches do the same for their coachees. They help them identify their goals and strengths, overcome limiting beliefs or other obstacles that hinder them from reaching their goals, and improve their well-being and performance.

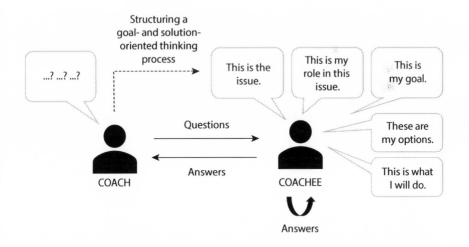

Figure 1 The essence of one-to-one coaching

Coaching does not necessarily need to be a formal process. Whenever you ask purposeful questions that help another person to think through a tricky problem and make progress in determining how to solve it, you are actually coaching (see Figure 1). Through answering the questions of the coach, the coachee will ideally find answers to their own 'big questions' in work and life.

How coaching differs from other developmental activities

Coaching is sometimes confused with other forms of developmental activities like counseling, psychotherapy, mentoring, career counseling, consulting, or teaching. Let us take a quick look at the differences.

- **Coaching is not counseling**. True, there are certain similarities. Both coaching and counseling are based on a one-to-one relationship in which the professional helps their client achieve higher levels of self-awareness and behavior change.[3] But while counseling is a form of 'talking therapy' in which exploration of a client's past can help them overcome personal problems, coaching is mainly future-oriented. It helps people develop their ability to reach their personal and work-related goals.
- **Coaching is not psychotherapy**. It is not a therapeutic intervention to cure mental health problems. Coaching focuses on personal development. It might tackle overcoming work or life-related problems, but it doesn't focus on mental health.
- **Coaching is not mentoring**. Mentoring is a long-term relationship in which a more experienced person, such as a member of the senior management team (the mentor), supports another person who has more recently started their career or joined a particular organization (the mentee) with advice and guidance, usually regarding their career development or the socialization process within the organization. Coaching, in turn, is a more structured and short-term intervention focused on reaching the coachee's specific development goals.
- **Coaching is not career counseling**. In career counseling, an individual's strengths, interests, and preferences are assessed in order to find a suitable job on the (external) job market. In contrast, coaching in a work context focuses on performance improvement in the current job.[4]

- **Coaching is not consulting**. Managers hire consultants to help them improve the performance of their organizations. Consultants are usually expected to be aware of industry best practices, share their experience, and provide professional advice on how to solve certain organizational challenges. They are paid for bringing answers. The role of a coach is different: rather than offering ready-made frameworks or solutions, coaches help coachees find their own solutions to their challenges by asking probing questions.
- **Coaching is not teaching**. In a teaching process, one person (the teacher) tries to transfer their knowledge or skills in a certain domain to another person (the learner). In a coaching relationship, it is assumed that the coachee is already in possession of the relevant knowledge and skills. Coaching is not about transferring knowledge. The role of the coach is to help the coachee recognize how they can best make use of their knowledge and skills in order to reach their personal and professional development goals.

EXERCISE

DISCOVER THE OUTCOMES OF COACHING

Find a person who has a coach. This could be any type of coach, such as a life coach, an executive coach, or maybe even a sports coach. Interview this person about the outcomes that coaching has had for them.

In what ways does the coach help this person to develop? What impact does the coach have on them? What is different now that they have a coach?

The outcomes of coaching

Is coaching really an effective method for helping people to develop? And what exactly are the outcomes that a coachee or an organization can expect from coaching?

Many researchers have tried to find answers to these questions. Overall, there is considerable evidence that most people who participate in coaching find it useful.[5] As Fillery-Travis and Lane conclude in their recent review of coaching research: "In all the studies undertaken, investigating whatever mode of coaching, the conclusion was the same—everyone likes to be coached and perceives that it impacts positively on their effectiveness."[6]

There are also indications that coaching produces **tangible results**, for example, in the form of higher work productivity or return on investment (ROI) for the organization.[7] Some studies show the ROI of coaching—the eventual financial benefits as a consequence of the coachee's improved work performance—as exceeding its costs by five times or even more.[8]

Here is a summary of research findings about the **outcomes that coaching can have for coachees** (see Figure 2):[9]

- **Focus.** Through the coaching process, coachees get a clearer focus on what they want to achieve and how they want to achieve it.
- **Increased motivation.** Having a coach as an accountability partner can provide coachees with additional motivation and encouragement to work on improving themselves and taking action to reach their goals.
- **Self-awareness and reflection.** Through the coaching process, coachees gain a clearer understanding of issues that are important to them. They can also become more aware of their own goals, strengths, and development needs.
- **Higher levels of self-confidence.** When coachees feel that they better understand an issue and how to deal with it, this can lead to improved confidence (a general trust in their own strengths) and self-efficacy (the feeling of being able to perform well in a specific task).
- **Well-being and work-related attitudes.** Research studies confirm that coaching in an organizational context can have a positive effect on a coachee's well-being and work-related attitudes, which can be of benefit for the client organization as well.

Research studies also report the following outcomes of coaching:[10]

- A **positive behavioral change** of coachees toward others.
- A higher degree of **goal attainment** and **enhanced work performance**.
- **Accelerated learning** and improved **problem-solving skills**.

- Enhanced **team performance** as a consequence of the improved **social and team leadership skills** of the coachee.
- **Personal development** including, for example, improved resilience, reduced stress levels, and a better work–life balance.

In addition, coachees benefit from the **feeling that they are being listened to** and from getting a chance to **see things in perspective.**[11]

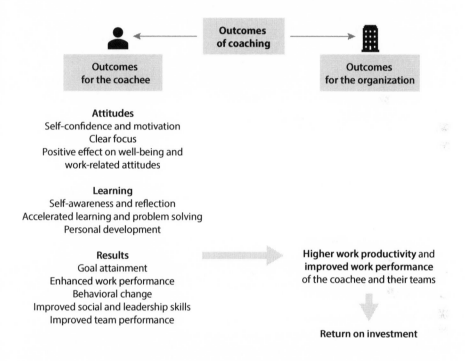

Figure 2 Overview of the main outcomes of coaching

Research also indicates that the benefits of coaching are more likely to be maintained in the workplace when coachees feel that both their managers and their peers care for their development and show interest in their coaching.[12]

One study reports that both coachees and human resource managers regard coaching as "the most effective method for altering a selected number of concrete management behaviors," especially compared to other management development methods like training courses, e-learning, job rotation or mentoring—despite the disadvantage of higher costs and a longer duration.[13]

For David B. Peterson, who conducted extensive research on coaching and served as senior director for executive coaching and leadership at Google, coaching is "one of the most potent, versatile, and efficient leadership development tools available."[14]

Life coaching

Life coaches help their coachees **enhance their well-being and attain greater fulfillment in their lives**. They use a goal- and solution-focused coaching approach similar to executive coaches, but have a broader focus that is not limited to an organizational or work context.

A life coach could, for example, use different assessment tools to explore which areas of their life coachees would like to work on or improve. One such tool is the **Wheel of Life**, in which coachees evaluate and rank their own satisfaction in different areas of their life, including health and fitness, family and friends, partner/spouse, money, career, living environment, recreation and leisure, and personal growth.[15]

The outcome of the self-assessment could then form the basis for setting improvement goals for particular areas of life, and for discussing options and action steps for implementing the improvements.

Life coaching often also focuses on identifying a coachee's **purpose in life** as well as their **strengths and passions**.[16] This could result in a **personal mission statement** (one or two sentences in which a person describes their purpose in life) and a reorientation of the coachee's activities to what brings them more joy and fulfillment in their life.

Designing an 'ideal life,' and then working with the coachee on closing the gaps between where they are now and where they want to be, is another approach to life coaching.[17] One tool that is sometimes used in this context is a **vision board**: a visual representation of the coachee's ideal life. It includes both images and words that represent the long-term goals of the coachee.[18]

The coachee might also already have a **concrete problem** in mind that they would like to discuss with a life coach. Together with the coach, they would then analyze their situation, set goals and develop action plans, try to find ways to overcome potential obstacles, and reflect on their behaviors and the outcomes of these behaviors.

Research shows that solution-focused life coaching has positive effects on **goal attainment, well-being, and quality of life**.[19] It has also been associated with higher levels of hope and decreased levels of depression in coachees.[20]

EXERCISE

YOUR PERSONAL MISSION STATEMENT

Step 1: Write down a personal mission statement—one or two sentences in which you describe what really matters in your life.

A few guiding questions that can help you with this task are: What are your biggest talents? What do you want to achieve in your life? Who do you want to be? What do you do with all your heart? For whom? (What is your impact on others?) And why do you want that?

Here are three examples of short personal mission statements:

- *"I am passionate about creating engaging and challenging learning experiences for my students to help them grow personally and become responsible and effective leaders who make a difference for the people they work with."*
- *"I use my positive attitude and energy to inspire my friends and colleagues to think in solutions rather than problems. In doing so, I spread hope and optimism."*
- *"I use my coaching skills to help others live the life that they aspire to."*

Step 2: Think about what you would need to do to fulfill your personal mission. Are there any goals that you want to set for yourself? Any obstacles that need to be overcome? Which actions will you still have to take to make it happen?

Step 3: If you have a learning partner, you can exchange your personal mission statements and interview each other on what you could do to turn your mission into reality.

COACHING FOR CLARITY AND DIRECTION

Kris de Jong is a professional life coach based in Auckland, New Zealand. He helps people who are dissatisfied with certain aspects of their life, who feel overwhelmed with work- or family-related pressures, or who want to gain more clarity on their direction in life.

This is how he summarizes his approach to life coaching: "I'll help you get clear on what's most important to you. Then we'll set real, achievable goals and develop a clear pathway to follow."

Here are the main steps of his coaching process (although he also customizes his approach based on the unique situation and needs of each individual client):

- Before the official coaching intervention starts, de Jong offers a free consultation session to find out more about the specific situation and requirements of the client.
- Based on a question and answer session, he creates what he calls a foundation document about the coachee's core values, personality, priorities, and ideal life. This acts as a reference point for the whole coaching process.
- He then clarifies which outcomes the coachee would like to achieve in which area of life (e.g. career, health/fitness, wealth, or lifestyle).
- The following coaching sessions are focused on optimizing the mindset of the coachee (identifying and overcoming limited beliefs), setting specific goals, devising smart strategies for reaching these goals, and minimizing or eliminating potential obstacles.
- After each session, the coachee receives a written weekly action plan with two to three action points, which are then reviewed at the beginning of the following session.
- After six to eight weekly one-hour coaching sessions, the coaching intervention ends with a summary and a discussion of concepts that the coachee can use in the future.

"If you don't have enough clarity you'll stay stuck … and frustrated," says de Jong. With his coaching, he supports his clients in gaining a new sense of direction and taking action to achieve what they really want out of life.

Source: www.eclipselifecoaching.com (accessed 8 February 2021). With kind permission of Kris de Jong.

Coaching in an organizational context

The rapid rise of the coaching industry in recent decades provides evidence for the increasing importance of coaching in organizations.

There are **different forms of coaching in organizations:**[21]

- Direct coaching of team members by their managers
- Coaching provided by trained internal coaches
- Coaching provided by professional external executive coaches

'**Manager-coaches**' use coaching skills to develop their team members, usually with the specific goal of improving work performance. In an internal study at Google, employees gave a clear answer when they were asked about the one most important behavior of a good manager: "is a good coach."[22] This is becoming even more relevant in a dynamic business environment, where people need to innovate and adapt their behaviors in order to keep up with disruptive change. In such an environment, according to London Business School Professor Herminia Ibarra and coaching expert Anne Scoular, managers "need to reinvent themselves as coaches whose job is to draw energy, creativity, and learning out of the people with whom they work."[23]

Trained internal coaches do not have a direct line management relationship with the coachee (i.e. they are not the coachee's boss). Yet they understand the organizational culture and are usually more accessible and affordable than external executive coaches. Structured internal coaching programs also offer the possibility to strengthen relationships between coaches and coachees from different departments. Furthermore, they can contribute to enhancing coaching skills—and therefore leadership skills—across the organization.

Professional **external executive coaches** come from different backgrounds. Some coaches are psychologists (who are trained, for example, in personality assessment and behavioral psychology). Other coaches have a background in business, management consulting, organization development, human resources, education, or sports.[24] Regardless of the discipline they come from, professional coaches are hired by organizations because of their expertise in supporting other people to develop themselves and improve their performance.

The professionalization of executive coaching

Since the 1980s, **executive coaching** has become a familiar term in the business environment. It describes a coaching setting in which the coachee is an 'executive'—a person with managerial responsibility in an organization. Executive coaching has increasingly been considered as a profession in its own right, with people trained in coaching skills offering their services to organizations.

In an executive coaching setting, there is usually a third party involved in addition to the coach and coachee: the coachee's **sponsoring organization,** typically represented by either the coachee's direct manager or a human resource manager. As the sponsoring organization eventually pays the bill, it will usually expect a return on investment for the coaching assignment.

Originally, professional coaching in an organizational context was often associated with getting people with a risk of derailing due to performance problems 'back on track.' It was often regarded as being similar to counseling, with the aim of removing work-related weaknesses or 'correcting' dysfunctional management behavior.[25] At that time, it was probably not the best sign when your manager said you were 'in need of a coach.'

It was soon noticed, however, that coaching could also be beneficial for people without major work-related deficits, and that it can actually be a highly effective development activity for both recently hired high-potential performers and well-established executives. If you are an executive who has a coach today, it is no longer seen as a sign of trouble, but rather as a kind of status symbol.[26]

Thus, what seemed to be just another management fad in the beginning turned out to become what is now widely considered as one of the most effective tools for developing people in organizations. As a consequence, executive coaching has become widespread throughout the corporate world and has grown into a **multibillion-dollar business**.[27]

The professionalization of the coaching industry also led to the emergence of different national and international **accreditation bodies**. These provide aspiring coaches with credentials for meeting certain professional standards following the successful completion of specific coaching training programs.

There is a large number of different certification institutions—around 50 in the UK alone, for example—which has created debates about their credibility and whether certifications are important at all.[28] Some of the most widely recognized international coaching accreditation bodies are the International Coach Federation (ICF), the International Association of Coaching (IAC), and the European Mentoring and Coaching Council (EMCC).

Another element of the professionalization of coaching is the emergence of **coaching supervision**. This is a formal process in which coaches get the opportunity to reflect on their professional practice and its challenges by working with experienced coaching supervisors.

The main purpose of supervision is to contribute to the continuing learning and development of professional coaches with the aim of improving the quality of their work.[29] There has been a rise in coaching supervision in some parts of the world in recent years, such as in the UK and other parts of Europe. The concept of supervision is less prevalent in other parts of the world, for example in North America.[30]

What executive coaches do

Why do organizations hire external executive coaches?

Basically, there are two different functions that an executive coach can fulfill:

- First, to **help an executive define and implement their own agenda**. 'Free agenda' coaching, however, involves the risk that it could also focus on areas that are actually less important for the organization.
- Second, to support individuals in their development process based on a **predefined and specific organizational agenda**.[31] In this case, the coaching will usually be focused on the development of skills that are particularly relevant for the organization. This could, for example,

include the aim to reach specific performance goals or to change certain behaviors of the executive.

In a survey conducted by *Harvard Business Review* among 140 executive coaches, the **six areas of assistance that executive coaches most frequently offer to coachees** were:[32]

1. Developing the capabilities of a high-potential manager
2. Facilitation of a transition
3. Acting as a sounding board on organizational dynamics
4. Discussing strategic matters
5. Addressing a 'derailing' behavior
6. Enhancing the interactions of a team

In another study, executive coaches reported that the most frequently addressed topics during their coaching sessions were leadership-related issues, the coachee's interpersonal skills and management style, communication issues, managing conflicts, and strategic thinking.[33]

The *Harvard Business Review* survey also reported that most professional executive coaching engagements have a **duration** between two and twelve months, with significantly shorter or longer coaching engagements being rare exceptions. When a number of coaching sessions are held over a period of several months, coachees have a chance to practice new approaches during that period, as well as to reflect on the outcomes and lessons learned with the coach.

At the heart of the coaching process are **coaching conversations**, in which the coach gives their full attention to the situation of the coachee. The role of the coach in these conversations is to ask probing questions that help the coachee:

- develop insight (get a clearer picture of the situation and their own role within it),
- create options for dealing with issues that they would like to tackle, and
- decide on which goals they want to set for themselves and which actions they are going to take to change the situation in a desired way.

The following **conversational techniques** are typically used by coaches to facilitate a good discussion in a coaching conversation:[34]

- Structuring the conversation in a goal-oriented way
- Asking the right questions
- Deep listening to better understand the coachee and their situation
- Making summaries of key aspects
- Sharing observations
- Providing constructive feedback

We will take a closer look at each of these techniques in Chapters 2 and 3.

It is also important for coaches to build rapport with their coachees and hold them accountable.[35] A **trusting relationship between coach and coachee** is highly important for being able to openly discuss sensitive issues. **Accountability**—asking the coachee to clearly express what they will do, and following up on what has really been done—translates coaching conversations into goal-directed action.[36]

Team coaching

Although we mainly focus on one-to-one coaching relationships in this book, there is also a 'one-to-many' or team coaching approach. In team coaching, the coach has a relationship and spends time with the team as a whole with the purpose of **developing the capacity of the team to perform well together**.

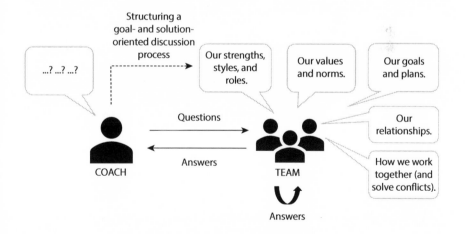

Figure 3 The essence of team coaching

Team coaching is usually either oriented toward supporting teams in defining and reaching their goals, or strengthening relationships and the capacity to perform as a team (see Figure 3).

Team coaches use coaching tools to **help a team**:

- identify and understand the strengths, styles, and team roles of the individual team members,
- define team values and norms,
- build trust within the team through open conversations,
- create a well-functioning collaboration process,
- set team goals and devise strategies and action plans for achieving those goals, and
- address and solve conflicts within the team.[37]

COACHING BEST PRACTICE

FILLING THE GAPS BETWEEN PEOPLE

Bill Campbell, a former football coach, became a mentor and executive coach of famous Silicon Valley entrepreneurs, including Apple's Steve Jobs and Google's Larry Page and Eric Schmidt. He emphasized the importance of team coaching. In his role as a team coach, he would usually focus on the team dynamics first before working on concrete problems.

Campbell described his approach in the following way: "I listen, observe, and fill the communication and understanding gaps between people."

He would try to make sure that the team was aligned around common goals. For example, at the beginning of a team coaching session, he would ask each team member to write down their top priority topics on a board, thus identifying overlaps and potential discrepancies. This could then form the basis for a coaching conversation about the team's joint goals and priorities, and how to achieve them.

Source: based on contents in Schmidt et al. (2019).

As in the case of one-to-one coaching, team coaches will usually refrain from offering advice on how to solve the team's issues, but will help the team to find their own answers instead.

Team coaching can have a positive impact on team performance as team members learn how to better combine their individual strengths. It can also enhance the satisfaction of team members when they experience a feeling of safety and support as a consequence of the open conversations that a coach facilitates within the team.[38]

Preconditions for effective coaching

What does it take for coaching to be effective? There are a few requirements that need to be fulfilled to ensure that a coaching process has a positive impact on the development of the coachee (see Figure 4):

- **Goal-orientation.** One recent review of the scientific literature on coaching concluded that "a solid focus on goals is most likely the key deciding factor in creating successful coaching interventions."[39] Research on goal setting shows that specific and at least somewhat challenging goals can have a strong motivational effect on people, especially when they are committed to these goals (which is usually the case when the goals are really relevant to them personally), and when there is a feedback mechanism in place that provides information about the extent to which a goal has been reached.[40] Effective coaches help coachees to formulate specific goals and identify the right courses of action that allow them to achieve their goals.
- **A good relationship between the coach and the coachee.** The quality of the relationship between the coach and coachee—including, in particular, a high level of trust, transparency, and mutually agreed goals—is a key factor in ensuring positive coaching outcomes.[41] In an organizational context, it is particularly important that the coachee sees the coach as an 'ally' and partner for their own development process, and not as a kind of 'spy' who is trying to gather information for their superiors. Confidentiality is therefore a key factor for a trusting coach–coachee relationship.
- **A coachable coachee.** The likelihood of a coaching intervention succeeding is also influenced by a coachee's attitudes toward coaching.

Figure 4 Preconditions for effective coaching

Their motivation and commitment to the coaching process, an expectation to get a positive outcome from it, and a belief in their own ability to tackle challenges and reach their goals (known as 'self-efficacy') can strongly contribute to positive outcomes.[42] A survey among executive coaches identified change readiness and active engagement as the most relevant factors for making a person coachable.[43]

- **A coachee who feels responsible**. Coaches cannot change the behavior of coachees. This is something that coachees can only do themselves. In order for coaching to be effective, coachees must therefore understand that they are responsible—for their choices, for their actions, and for the outcomes of their actions. A coach can help them to think through an issue and devise action plans, but ultimately, it is the coachee who is in control and who needs to feel responsible for their own situation and actions.[44]

- **A collaborative mindset**. As mentioned before, coaching is neither teaching nor mentoring. It is not about a more knowledgeable person advising another person how they could—or should—handle a certain situation. Ideally, it is a partnership of equals, in which both the coach and coachee have a collaborative mindset. Coach and coachee work together with the aim of helping the coachee gain their own insights and make their own choices about which actions to take. Therefore, in a coaching relationship, a coachee should neither feel dominated nor controlled by the coach.[45]

Personal development is a journey, and a coach is the coachee's travel companion on that journey. Every coaching journey has a destination—a goal that the coachee wants to achieve, a situation they want to improve, or a behavior they want to change. But the journey is its own reward too, where the coach and coachee create insights together and learn from each other.

WHAT IS COACHING? A BRIEF SUMMARY IN 10 POINTS

1. A **coach** is a person who helps another person (the coachee) become more effective in their life and work.

2. The coach's main tools are **intelligent questions** that help the coachee to think through challenging issues, raise their self-awareness, consider their options, and take the right actions to achieve their performance and development goals.

3. Coaching clearly **differs from other developmental interventions** like counseling, psychotherapy, mentoring, career counseling, consulting, or teaching.

4. Coaching can have a range of **positive outcomes** for both the coachee (e.g. increased self-awareness, confidence, motivation, focus, goal attainment, and personal development) and the sponsoring organization, which profits from the skills and performance improvement of the coachee.

5. **Life coaches** help their coachees enhance their well-being and attain greater fulfillment in their lives.

6. In an **organizational context**, coaching (which can be provided either by 'manager-coaches,' trained internal coaches, or professional external coaches) is oriented toward helping coachees become more effective in their organizational role.

7. **Executive coaching** has established a reputation as a highly effective development activity in organizations.

8. At the heart of the coaching process are **coaching conversations**, in which the coach supports the coachee in analyzing issues that are important to them, setting goals, creating and evaluating options, and developing concrete action plans for reaching their goals.

9. In **team coaching**, coaches support teams in defining and reaching their goals as well as in strengthening working relationships within the team.

10. There are a few important **preconditions for coaching to be effective**: goal-orientation, a good relationship between the coach and coachee, a coachable coachee, the coachee taking responsibility, and a collaborative mindset.

Notes for Chapter 1

1   Gates (2013).
2   Whiterspoon & White (1996).
3   Joo (2005).
4   Feldman & Lankau (2005).
5   Bono et al. (2009), p. 363.
6   Fillery-Travis & Lane (2021), p. 61.
7   Fillery-Travis & Lane (2021).
8   Peterson (2011).
9   Athanasopoulou & Dopson (2018); Bachkirova et al. (2021); Burt & Talati (2017); Evers et al. (2006); Grant (2003); Rekalde et al. (2017); Starr (2016); Sue-Chan & Latham (2004); Wasylyshyn (2003).
10 Athanasopoulou & Dopson (2018); Bachkirova et al. (2021); Burt & Talati (2017); Evers et al. (2006); Grant (2003); Rekalde et al. (2017); Starr (2016); Sue-Chan & Latham (2004); Wasylyshyn (2003).
11 Bachkirova et al. (2021).
12 Stewart et al. (2021).
13 Rekalde et al. (2017).
14 Peterson (2011), p. 556.
15 Vickers & Bavister (2010).
16 Stoltzfus (2008).
17 Stoltzfus (2008).
18 Belton (2020).
19 Grant (2003).
20 Green et al. (2007).
21 Fillery-Travis & Lane (2021).
22 Garvin (2013).
23 Ibarra & Scoular (2019), p. 119.
24 Feldman & Lankau (2005); Peterson (2011).
25 McCauley & Hezlett (2001).
26 Bono et al. (2009).
27 Athanasopoulou & Dopson (2018).
28 Scoular (2009).
29 Hawkins (2014).
30 Tkach & Di Giolamo (2021).
31 Fillery-Travis & Lane (2021).
32 Kauffmann & Coutu (2008).
33 Bono et al. (2009).
34 Starr (2016).
35 Bono et al. (2009).
36 Whitmore (2017).
37 Britton (2015).
38 Dimas et al. (2016).
39 Grant & O'Connor (2019), p. 7
40 Locke (2006).
41 Grant & O'Connor (2019); Kauffman & Coutu (2008); Lai & Palmer (2019).
42 Athanasopoulou & Dopson (2018); Stewart et al. (2021).
43 Kauffman & Coutu (2008).
44 Whitmore (2017).
45 Starr (2016).

2

EFFECTIVE COACHING CONVERSATIONS

This chapter will enable you to

» Structure a coaching conversation in a goal- and solution-oriented way.
» Apply the GROW model, one of the most widely used coaching frameworks.
» Ask coaching questions that help a coachee identify their goals, analyze their current situation, develop alternative strategies for making progress, and commit to concrete action steps.
» Use a cognitive behavioral coaching approach to help a coachee adopt a positive mindset for change.

The core of the coaching process are coaching conversations. These are primarily **focused on the coachee** and the issues that are challenging and important for them. The aim of a coaching conversation is to **support the coachee** in their thinking and learning process. Coaches help their coachees identify the right steps they need to take to address their challenges and reach their goals.

A coaching conversation can also be seen as a **process of enquiry**, in which the coach facilitates the coachee's learning and development through asking questions in a structured, solution-oriented process.

A typical coaching session starts—after a warm-up phase with the usual courtesies and checking whether the coachee is fully present and ready for the conversation—with a review of the previous session and an update of what has happened between the sessions (*"Let us first take a look at what you decided to do last time"*). This is usually followed by jointly defining the goals for the current session (*"What would you like us to focus on today?"*).

The main part of the coaching session then usually consists of the actual **coaching conversation**, based on a discussion of the topics that are relevant to the coachee. In this conversation, the coach helps the coachee to explore problem situations in more depth, identify options for dealing with these problems, and develop an action plan for making progress.

GROW—A widely used coaching framework

"If a coach can't tell you what methodology he uses—what he does and what outcomes you can expect—show him the door," advises Anne Scoular, the co-founder of a coaching institute and an associate scholar at Oxford University's Saïd Business School.[1]

A methodology that is widely used by coaches around the world for structuring their coaching conversations is the **GROW model** (see Figure 5).[2]

GROW stands for:

- Goal: *What does the coachee want to achieve?*
- Reality: *What does the current situation look like?*
- Options: *What are the alternative courses of action for improving the situation?*
- Will: *What will the coachee actually do to improve the situation? Which concrete action steps will they take?*

The model is simple yet also very powerful, as is forces the coachee to systematically examine an issue in a goal-oriented way, identify and weigh several options, and make decisions about the right way forward. Ideally, the coachee then also feels accountable for implementing their decisions.

Let us now take a closer look at each of the four steps of the GROW model.

Figure 5 The GROW model[22]

Goal: What does the coachee want to achieve?

In essence, coaching is a **goal-oriented process**. The coachee would like to achieve something. That's why they turn to a coach in the first place. It is therefore important for the coach and coachee to form a clear common understanding of what the coachee would actually like to accomplish.

Counterintuitively, **goal setting comes before the reality check** in the GROW model. Sir John Whitmore, who first published the model in the early 1990s, explains that when we base our goals on the current reality, we tend to come up with responses that are "limited by past performance, lacking in creativity due to simple extrapolation," which can then also result in "smaller increments than may be achievable."[3]

The idea behind putting the goal-setting phase before the reality check is to not limit yourself too early or become too fixated on 'what is' as opposed to what could be achieved. Coachees increase their chances of making significant progress when they think about more stretching goals and ideal outcomes first before chaining themselves to the constraints of their current reality.

There are two different **types of goals** that coaches need to be aware of:

- Inspirational **end goals**—what the coachee would (finally) like to achieve in the long term
- Specific **performance goals**—concrete levels of performance for certain activities that bring the coachee closer to reaching their end goal[4]

The end goal for a professional tennis player, for example, could be to win a Grand Slam tournament within the next five years. Their concrete performance goal for the next three months could be to get 95 percent of the balls within the lines when they serve.

Note that performance goals are usually more in a person's control than end goals. By definition, performance goals depend primarily on one's own performance, while end goals are usually also influenced by other (non-controllable) circumstances.

Performance goals are 'doing goals'—they relate to something that the coachees are actually able to do themselves. Many coaching experts say that performance goals should be **SMART**—**s**pecific, **m**easurable, **a**greed (instead of imposed), **r**ealistic (but still challenging), and **t**imely (with a clearly defined target date).

To have a stronger motivational effect, it is preferable to formulate performance goals with a **positive instead of a negative focus** (e.g. *"To improve my tennis serve skills"* instead of *"To make less mistakes when I serve"*).

As an **outcome of the goal-setting phase** of a GROW conversation, both the coach and coachee should reach a joint understanding about:

a. the end goal that the coachee wants to reach,
b. the performance goals (ideally not more than three) that the coachee needs to achieve in order to be able to reach the end goal, and
c. the concrete goal for (or focus of) the current coaching session.

Letting the coachee voice their goals is a key first step for enabling positive change and transition, as the coachee will gain clarity about their desired future state—and ideally about why this is important for them.[5] It is then easier to keep the discussion goal-focused in the next steps of the coaching process, and to help the coachee identify what they will actually do in order to reach their goals.

Before discussing different options for reaching a particular goal, however, the coach and coachee need to come to a common understanding about the current situation.

COACHING QUESTIONS

COACHING QUESTIONS FOR THE 'GOAL' STAGE

Questions related to setting goals for the current coaching session:

- "What would you like to achieve with today's discussion?"
- "What would be a good outcome for you of our conversation?"
- "What is the most important thing that you would like to talk about today?"
- "You seem to have different goals here. Which one do you want us to focus on?"
- "What specifically is it about this issue that you would like to discuss?"
- "Is there anything else that you would like us to work on?"

Questions related to the end goal:

- "What exactly would you like to have accomplished in three months/ a year/…?"
- "What is your ultimate goal? What would your life look like if you had achieved it?"
- "What makes this goal so important for you?"
- "How would things be different if you had achieved your goal?"
- "What will your new life look like?"
- "What is in for you personally when you achieve that?"

Questions related to the performance goal:

- "What is it—very specifically—that you would need to accomplish first as a precondition for reaching your end goal?"

- "What are the main milestones on the way to achieving this goal? When would you need to reach them by?"
- "How could you set a goal in a way that it primarily depends on your actions and performance rather than on the circumstances or what others do?"
- "How will you know that you have achieved your performance goal? How will you measure success?"

Reality: What does the current situation look like?

Step 2 in the GROW model is about **getting a clear understanding of the starting point** in the issue that the coachee wants to discuss.

The main aim of this phase is to **objectively assess the situation** together. 'Objective' means that the coach and coachee should strive to establish the facts rather than just rely on personal feelings about what seems 'right' or 'wrong' about a certain situation.

Coaches can support an objective inquiry through asking coachees to explain what happened and **present the facts** without evaluating or judging them.

For example, coaches can ask questions such as:

- What exactly happened?
- What is the coachee's role in the situation?
- Who else is involved in the situation? What were the actions of the main protagonists? What are their interests and (potential) motives for acting in a certain way?
- What has the coachee (or others) already done—and what were the results?
- Which obstacles have hindered progress so far?

The **role of the coachee** is particularly important in this context. With a question like *"In what way did your actions contribute to these results?"* a coach can try to establish a link between concrete behaviors of the coachee and the outcomes of these behaviors. This can help to increase coachees' **self-awareness**. They will be able to better understand their own role in a certain situation and perceive themselves as active agents rather than passive 'victims'.

It is also important to acknowledge that there is an **external reality** (e.g. certain power relationships, other people's attitudes and actions, group norms, or processes within an organization) on the one hand, and the coachee's **internal reality** (e.g. personal values, expectations, attitudes, or feelings) on the other hand.[6] Both realities can potentially play an important role for resolving an issue. It therefore makes sense to explore both, too.

One important part of a coachee's internal reality are **anxieties and fears**—both open or hidden ones. Many people are reluctant to act because they fear negative consequences: failing, losing something that they value, upsetting others, being ridiculed, being rejected, or being seen as a fraud, to name just a few examples.[7] For a coachee, understanding their fears is the first step toward accepting and overcoming them. That is why coaches often spend considerable time exploring this 'darker side' of their coachees' internal reality.

"Great coaches sniff out hidden truths," wrote executive coaching experts Stratford Sherman and Alyssa Freas in an article for *Harvard Business Review*, adding that they are able to "turn over rocks" and find out more about the underlying issues that are not openly addressed by the coachee.[8]

During the 'Reality' phase, the conversation should stay in an **enquiry mode** instead of jumping to a 'quick fix' solution. Coaches need to strike a balance between keeping the conversation goal-focused and progress-oriented, and missing out important parts of the exploration process because there has been too much focus on getting immediate 'results.'[9]

COACHING QUESTIONS

COACHING QUESTIONS FOR THE 'REALITY' STAGE

Questions related to the external reality:

- "What is happening right now?"
- "What are the main factors that contributed to this situation?"
- "What other factors might be involved here?"
- "Who else is involved in this issue? What is their role?"
- "Who else is affected? In what way?"

- "Which steps have you already taken to tackle this issue?"
- "What happened as a consequence?"
- "What are the main obstacles?"
- "What stops you from …?"
- "What resources are needed?"

Questions related to the coachee's internal reality:

- "On a scale of 1 to 10, how important is XY for you?"
- "What makes this important for you?"
- "How would you describe your emotions when XY happened?"
- "How does XY affect you?"
- "What are your expectations regarding XY?"
- "What fears do you have regarding XY?"
- "What are your main concerns?"
- "What holds you back from taking action?"

Some experienced coaches suggest avoiding 'Why' questions, as in *"Why did you do this?"* The reason for avoiding such questions is that they might put the coachee in a defensive mode in which they feel the need to justify their actions instead of staying focused on objectively exploring what happened.

Only if both sides feel they have gained a clear picture about the situation is it time to move on to the 'Options' stage of the GROW model.

Options: What are the alternative courses of action?

The aim of the 'Options' phase in a GROW conversation is to **generate a range of different alternatives for reaching the coachee's goal**.

It is the time for the coach and coachee to be creative. During this phase, it is important not to limit oneself too early with restrictive thinking. Thoughts like *"This cannot be implemented because …"*, *"They would never do this"*, or *"We do not have enough resources"* should be suspended for the moment.

Instead of reinforcing existing obstacles, the focus should lie on identifying potential ways to **remove obstacles**. Thinking about options that the coachee would have if certain restrictions (e.g. regarding money, time, or other resources) did not exist can lead to more creative solutions.

The coach can contribute to the **generation of options** in two ways: first, by asking questions that elicit more ideas from the coachee, and second, by contributing their own ideas to trigger more associations and thoughts on the coachee's side.

Proficient coaches, however, only forward their own ideas when two conditions are fulfilled:

1. The coachee cannot find new solutions any more
2. The coach has asked the coachee for permission before sharing their ideas (*"I also have some ideas here. Would you like me to share them with you?"*)

Having more options to evaluate and choose from is obviously better than being stuck with only one option. But the coach and coachee should also **avoid information overload.** It is usually difficult to process more than five serious options in a meaningful discussion. This does not mean that creating more than five options is not sometimes a good idea, too. But after some brainstorming, it is necessary to **narrow the options space** to the few most promising ideas.

Once all options are on the table, the coach can summarize them (which is a lot easier when the coach is also taking notes during the conversation) and then ask the coachee **which options they want to prioritize.**

This stage can also involve an exploration of the **main advantages and disadvantages of the most promising options.**

COACHING QUESTIONS

COACHING QUESTIONS FOR THE 'OPTIONS' STAGE

Questions related to generating different courses of action:

- "What could be a potential solution here?"
- "What choices do you have?"
- "What steps could you take to make progress in this issue?"

- "Let us try to explore another course of action. What else could you do about this?"
- "What advice would you give to someone else in the same situation as you?"
- "What did you do when you were in a similar situation before?"
- "And what else?"[23]

Questions related to overcoming restrictions:

- "What would happen if this obstacle could be removed?"
- "What could you do to remove this obstacle?"
- "How could this risk be reduced?"
- "What stops you from doing this?"
- "How would you proceed if you had more money/time/information ...?"
- "Who could help you here? Who knows more about this? Who has done something like this before?"
- "If <admired person XY> were in your shoes, what would they do?"

Questions related to prioritizing options:

- "May I offer a summary of the options that we discussed? Which of these options do you see as the most promising one?"
- "What are the most important advantages of following this option?"
- "What are the main risks involved in following this option?"
- "On a scale of 1–10, how confident are you that you could succeed with this course of action?"
- "What would you need to get your confidence level up to a 9 or 10?"

Will: Which concrete action steps will the coachee take?

In the final phase of a GROW conversation, attention shifts from exploring options to **making a decision** and **developing an action plan**.

When coachees weigh the advantages and disadvantages of their options, they are in a **'deliberative' mindset**. When they know what they will do and focus on getting it done, they are in an **'implemental' mindset**.[10] The coach's aim in this last phase of the coaching conversation is to help the coachee make the transition from a deliberative to an implemental mindset.

'Will' refers to a concrete will—or intention—of the coachee to **take certain actions**. As an outcome of this phase, the coachee should ideally:

- decide *what* they will do,
- define a specific timeframe (*when* they will do it),
- plan how they will do it (*which concrete steps* they will take), and
- have an idea about how they will *overcome potential obstacles* in implementing their planned actions.

The coachee makes a commitment to themselves and to the coach at that stage. Through clearly stating what they will do and by when they will do it, they become **accountable**.

The coach's job is not to push their coachee in a certain direction here, but to support them in finding their own way forward and creating their own concrete, realistic, and workable action plan.

COACHING BEST PRACTICE

HELPING A COACHEE TO BREAK THROUGH THEIR OWN LIMITATIONS

Karen Morley is an executive coach and author from Melbourne, Australia. "As coach," she says, "I take responsibility for helping to identify new actions and approaches, and reviewing them, and ensure accountability against the agreed goals."

For Morley, coaching is "a fine balance between challenge and support." She supports her clients, for example, through acknowledging efforts and appreciating insights, and challenges them "mainly through asking questions and presenting different ways to see things."

She sees coaching conversations as a way to self-discovery and an opportunity "to step out of constraints and to imagine your ideal self."

In one example, she worked with her client Felicity, who felt unsure about her readiness to take on further leadership responsibility. Morley tried to explore with Felicity what kind of leader she wanted to be, and then asked her, "What's stopping you from doing it your way?"

She thus helped Felicity discover her identity first. In the following step, she made her client realize that it was actually in her own hands to become the leader she wanted to be. With these insights, says Morley, "Felicity was able to break through her own limitations." As a result of the coaching intervention, Felicity became highly effective in her new leadership role.

Source: https://www.karenmorley.com.au/leadership-coaching-approach/ and https://www.karenmorley.com.au/motivate-lasting-change/ (accessed 29 January 2021). With kind permission of Karen Morley.

In the 'Will' phase, the coach can probe whether the coachee's planned actions will really be instrumental for reaching their goals. A coach can also help the coachee assess their own level of commitment to the action plan.

At the end of the conversation, a coach will typically **summarize the main points** that were discussed and agreed.

An important step to increasing commitment is to write down the planned actions and agreed deadlines on a **'next steps list'** or **action memo** (see Chapter 5 for details). If the coach is taking notes, the coachee should first read and confirm the action memo before it is 'officially' sent (for example in an email) to the coachee.[11]

The action memo serves as a record of the points that were agreed, and is also used as a starting point for the next coaching session.

COACHING QUESTIONS

COACHING QUESTIONS FOR THE 'WILL' STAGE

Questions related to setting up an action plan:

- "What will you do?"
- "Which option will you pursue to achieve your goal?"
- "Which concrete action steps will you take?"
- "What will be your next step to make it happen?"
- "When (exactly) will you do this?"

- "When will you put this into practice?"
- "How will this action help you to achieve your goal?"
- "Whose support do you need to make it happen? What exactly will you do (and when) to get that support?"
- "What are the main obstacles that you expect to face when you implement your actions?
- "How will you overcome these obstacles?"

Questions related to checking the level of commitment:

- "On a scale of 1–10, how committed are you to taking this step?"
- "What would you have to change to turn your commitment from 7 to 10?"

EXERCISE

USE THE GROW MODEL IN AN INFORMAL CONVERSATION

Next time a friend, colleague, or family member is complaining about something, try not to give them your advice, but help them find their own answer.

Follow the GROW model and ask questions through which they can:

- express what they would like to change (G),
- clarify the situation (e.g. key facts, potential causes and influences) (R),
- think about their options (O), and
- say what they will do about it in a concrete way (W).

This is not a formal coaching session, of course, so do not expect that you will perfectly cover all steps of the process. Maybe your conversational partner is not in the mood to explore the situation or think seriously about their options. In such a case, do not put pressure on them. Just try to focus on asking purpose-based questions instead of stating your own view and offering advice right away.

Other coaching models

Although the GROW model is used by many coaches around the world, there are also several other approaches to structuring coaching conversations. Many of them are actually quite similar to the GROW model.

Let us take a look at Peter Hawkins's **CLEAR framework** as one example:[12]

- Contract—agree on what the coachee wants to discuss and achieve in the coaching session.
- Listen—ask questions to develop a good understanding of the issue that the coachee wants to discuss.
- Explore—dig deeper to help the coachee identify what they would like to change and why, what a desired future state could look like, and what options they have to handle the situation.
- Actions—set up a concrete action plan (what will the coachee do to reach the desired future state).
- Review—assess the progress that has been made on what the coachee wanted to achieve.

Whatever framework you use, they all share a common purpose: helping the coach and coachee structure their conversations in a way that includes a thorough analysis of the situation, establishing clarity about what the coachee wants to achieve, exploring the options that the coachee has to reach their goals, and agreeing on a concrete action plan.

Cognitive behavioral coaching

Another approach to structuring coaching conversations that is frequently used by psychologically trained coaches, in particular, is **cognitive behavioral coaching (CBC)**.[13]

CBC is based on **cognitive behavioral theory (CBT)**, one of the most widely studied and used approaches to psychotherapy.

When people are faced with a new and difficult situation, they typically respond in three different ways:[14]

- **Physical responses** (e.g. an increased heart rate or blood pressure)
- **Intellectual responses** (e.g. a rational internal evaluation of the situation, weighing the pros and cons)
- **Emotional responses** (with either positive or negative feelings)

These internal responses, in turn, strongly determine the subsequent behavioral response.

CBT postulates that it is often not an adverse event in our life that causes the most trouble for us, but the way we interpret such an event (i.e. our intellectual and emotional responses to what happened).

Albert Ellis, one of the main proponents of CBT, has explained this phenomenon with his **ABC model**:

- **a**dversity, a difficult situation that we encounter in our life (A), *leads to*
- **b**eliefs that we form about the adversity (B), *which in turn leads to*
- certain emotional and behavioral **c**onsequences (C).[15]

In short: it is not the situation itself but our thoughts about it that directly influence our emotional state and behavior.

Imagine, for example, that you are a sales manager who just lost a major customer (this is the adversity, A). If you then start to worry that losing the customer could mean you will miss your sales targets and maybe even lose your job (this is your belief about the adversity, B), you would probably feel anxiety and experience higher stress levels (these are the emotional consequences, C).[16]

As it is not the adversity itself that leads to the negative emotional consequences, but rather a person's beliefs about the adversity, this suggests they can also do something about it.

A person can, for example, use the **ABCDE model** instead of being stuck with ABC thinking (see Figure 6). The 'DE' part is the core of the coaching intervention. If a person **d**isputes their existing beliefs (D), develops different beliefs, and realizes that they could also take a different (and more productive) perspective on the adversity, they open the door for an exchange of the existing negative interpretation with a new, more effective outlook (E).[17]

In the example above, the sales manager could also think about the situation in the following way: *"There are other ways to reach our sales budgets, too. Let us learn about the reasons why our customers leave, and then create and implement a new customer retention strategy that will also impress our top management team."*

This would be a much more productive response to the situation than just feeling anxious about all the bad things that could happen as a consequence of losing a customer.

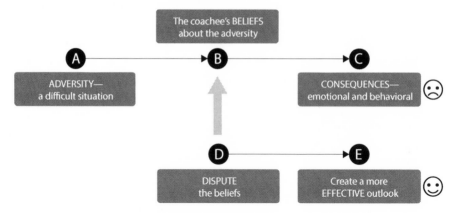

Figure 6 The ABCDE model of cognitive behavioral coaching[24]

Based on CBT, cognitive behavioral coaching focuses on **making coachees aware of their negative beliefs** and helping them to explore different options for interpreting their situation in a more positive way.[18]

Through challenging self-defeating thoughts and gaining a better understanding of the reciprocal links between the environment on the one hand and their own beliefs, feelings, and behavior on the other hand, coachees are empowered to find new solutions for their problems and attain their goals.[19]

Here is an example of a process model for a **coaching conversation that follows the cognitive behavioral coaching approach** (see Figure 7):[20]

1. **Context**: Examine the current (problem) situation and its context.
2. **Vision**: Determine what an ideal future looks like for the coachee.
3. **Current beliefs and behaviors**: Identify thoughts and behaviors that might not be helpful if the coachee wants to achieve their vision; raise the coachee's awareness of the link between thoughts, behaviors, and outcomes.
4. **Vision-focused beliefs and behaviors**: Explore beliefs and behaviors that would be helpful for achieving the coachee's vision.
5. **Experiment**: Encourage the coachee to try out different thinking strategies (e.g. monitoring and recording their thoughts, or focusing on what they learn from a certain situation instead of thinking about all the bad things that can happen), and to try out different behaviors (e.g. trying

out a questioning instead of telling approach when delegating a task to a team member). The results of these 'experiments' are then evaluated in the following coaching session.

6. **Consolidate**: Help the coachee independently monitor and adapt their thought and behavioral patterns (e.g. create a self-check tool together with the coachee).

A coaching conversation that follows this model can help a coachee to understand the role of their own thoughts and beliefs in facilitating or hindering their ability to reach their goals.

Frameworks like the GROW model or cognitive behavioral coaching provide a solution-oriented focus for coaching conversations. They can therefore help a coachee establish a "positive mindset for change."[21]

These process models, however, do not need to be slavishly followed. The models are not an end in themselves, but only tools that can be flexibly adapted based on the concrete requirements of the coachee.

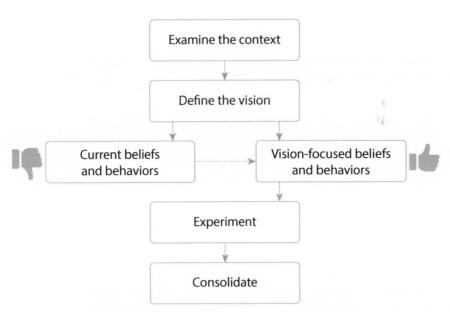

Figure 7 A process model of cognitive behavioral coaching[25]

COACHING QUESTIONS FOR COGNITIVE BEHAVIORAL COACHING (FOLLOWING THE ABCDE MODEL)

Questions related to exploring the adversity (A):

- "Can you give me the main facts about what happened in this situation?"
- "Could you describe the situation that caused the problem?"
- "Who (else) was involved, and what role did they play?"

Questions related to understanding the current beliefs and thoughts of the coachee (B):

- "What were your first thoughts when this happened?"
- "Did this incident keep you awake at night? What were your thoughts?"
- "What are you saying to yourself about it?"
- "What do you think are the main consequences of this event?"
- "What image do you hold in your head of what happened?"
- "What other thoughts do you have about this?"

Questions related to understanding emotional and behavioral consequences (C):

- "How did/do you feel about what happened in this situation?"
- "On a scale of 1 to 10, how strong are these feelings?"
- "Did you notice any bodily reactions when this happened (e.g. sweating or a higher pulse rate)?"
- "How did you react to what happened?"
- "In what way did you change your behavior after this?"
- "What are the positive and/or negative outcomes of your behavior?"

Questions related to disputing beliefs about adversity (D):

- "How do you know that this is true?"
- "Is this a fact or an opinion?"
- "What is the evidence that backs up your thoughts?"
- "Are there any facts that might contradict your thoughts about this?"

- "Which assumptions are your thoughts based on? Can we explore these assumptions in more detail?"
- "What is the worst-case scenario here? Can you cope with the worst case?"
- "What could happen in the best case?"
- "Does A necessarily lead to B? Or could there be other outcomes, too?"
- "Is there a disadvantage of thinking about the situation in this way?"
- "What is the likelihood (between 0 and 100 percent) that this is really going to happen?"
- "What other perspective could another person have on the situation?"
- "Did you include all the facts when you formed this belief?"
- "Does this thought help you to reach your goals?"

Questions related to creating a new, more effective outlook (E):

- "Is there a different way of interpreting this situation?"
- "Given that the facts stand as they are, what could you do to make the best out of this situation?"
- "What kind of beliefs or behaviors would help you here if you want to achieve your goals?"
- "Think about a person who you admire. What would this person think or do if they were in the same situation?"
- "What else could you do to cope with the situation?"

Source: partly inspired by Ackerman (2020) and Williams & Palmer (2018).

APPLY THE ABCDE MODEL TO YOUR OWN SITUATION

Step 1: Try to use the ABCDE method to analyze a difficult or unpleasant situation you have experienced in the recent past.

Write down short answers to the following questions:

- What happened in this situation? (A)
- How did you interpret it? Can you remember any negative self-talk or beliefs that you had about it? (B)
- How did you feel as a consequence of your interpretation of the situation? How did you adapt your behavior? (C)
- Could you have used an alternative way of thinking about what happened? (Use some of the coaching questions related to disputing beliefs about adversity here.) (D)
- Which beliefs and behaviors could have been more effective for ensuring a positive outcome in this situation? (E)

Step 2: Reflect on what you learned from this exercise. Did it open your mind to different ways of thinking and reacting to a difficult situation? How could you use your learnings in future coaching conversations?

RECOGNIZING THE LIMITATIONS OF COACHING PROCESS MODELS

Melanie Allen is a life and executive coach based in Leeds, UK. Although she uses several tools and techniques based on different theoretical traditions, she is also aware of the limitations of following structured goal-oriented coaching models.

"A completely action-centered approach, where we make a structured plan and follow it, doesn't suit everyone and every situation," she says. Instead, she prefers what she calls "a more 'inside out' approach," in which she first explores her coachees' perceptions and attitudes with them before working on concrete action plans and behavior change.

"Small insights and shifts of perspective will naturally lead to changing what you do (action) and can have a huge effect on your life," she says. "I've nothing against plans, and they are very useful in some circumstances, particularly in the shorter term. But I like to keep … [the coachee]—rather than the plan—at the center of the coaching."

Although Allen also works with clear goals and structured plans—especially in the short-term and when the coachee wants to make progress on a concrete single issue—she generally regards a combination of aims and a flexible strategy as more effective in the long term.

Source: http://www.melanieallen.co.uk/coaching-approach/ (accessed 29 January 2021). With kind permission of Melanie Allen (www.melanieallen.co.uk).

EFFECTIVE COACHING CONVERSATIONS:
A BRIEF SUMMARY IN 10 POINTS

1. Coaching conversations are **primarily focused on the coachee** and the issues that are important to them.

2. Typical coaching sessions **begin with a review** of what has happened since the previous session and an **agreement on the goals** for the current session.

3. The **core of a coaching session** usually consists of a structured discussion on what the coachee wants to achieve, what the current situation looks like, and what the coachee could and will do to make progress toward reaching their goals.

4. One of the most widely used frameworks for structuring coaching conversations is the **GROW model** (Goal, Reality, Options, Will).

5. The aim of the **'Goal' phase** is to clarify which long-term end goals and specific short-term performance goals the coachee wants to achieve.

6. During the **'Reality' phase**, the coach and coachee try to objectively assess the situation of the coachee, taking into account both the external reality and the coachee's internal reality.

7. Different alternatives for reaching the coachee's goals are explored in the **'Options' phase**.

8. In the **'Will' phase**, coachees translate their favored option for making progress into concrete, committed action.

9. Many coaches also use **cognitive behavioral coaching (CBC)** as a basic approach for structuring coaching conversations. CBC focuses on making coachees aware of potentially unhelpful beliefs and creating a more positive and solution-oriented attitude.

10. One tool that can be used in CBC is the **ABCDE model**. Following this model, the coachee first describes the **a**dversity (a difficult situation they are faced with), their **b**eliefs about it, and any emotional and behavioral **c**onsequences [ABC]. The coach then helps the coachee **d**ispute unhelpful beliefs and develop a more **e**ffective, forward-looking outlook [DE].

Notes for Chapter 2

1   Scoular (2009), p. 96.
2   Whitmore (2017).
3   Whitmore (2017), p. 98.
4   Whitmore (2017).
5   Grant (2021).
6   Whitmore (2017).
7   Belton (2020).
8   Sherman & Freas (2004), p. 87.
9   Starr (2016).
10 Gollwitzer (1996).
11 Whitmore (2017).
12 Hawkins & Smith (2013).
13 Lai & Palmer (2019).
14 Natale & Diamante (2005).
15 Ellis (1994).
16 Sternad (2020).
17 Neenan (2008).
18 Good et al. (2013).
19 Grant (2017).
20 Adapted from Good et al. (2013) and Williams & Palmer (2018).
21 Lai & Palmer (2019), p. 158.
22 Graphical representation by the author inspired by concepts in Whitmore (2017); illustration source: pixabay.com.
23 Michael Bungay Stanier (2016), a bestselling author on coaching, considers "And what else?" to be the most powerful coaching question of all.
24 Graphical representation by the author inspired by concepts in Ellis (1994).
25 Graphical representation by the author inspired by concepts in Good et al. (2013) and Williams & Palmer (2018).

3

THE COACHING PROCESS

This chapter will enable you to

» Organize a professional coaching process.
» Define the purpose and goals of a coaching intervention together with a client.
» Explain what a coach needs to consider for building a positive relationship with both the client organization and the coachee.
» Use assessment tools, progress reviews, and structured reflection and evaluation to improve the quality of the coaching process.

Coaching is a process. By definition, every process consists of a series of actions that lead to a desired result—in our case, helping a coachee reach their goals and realize their full potential.

Coaching conversations, which we already explored in Chapter 2, are the heart of the coaching process. But they are not the only part of the process.

A typical **executive coaching process** in a professional organizational context includes the following phases (see Figure 8):

1. Defining the purpose of the coaching intervention
2. Building the relationship with the organization
3. Building the relationship with the coachee
4. Gathering and analyzing data
5. Coaching sessions (in which the actual coaching conversations take place)
6. Progress reviews (follow-ups) to ensure accountability
7. Reflection and evaluation of the coaching process

In this chapter, we will take a closer look at what happens in each of these seven phases of the coaching process.

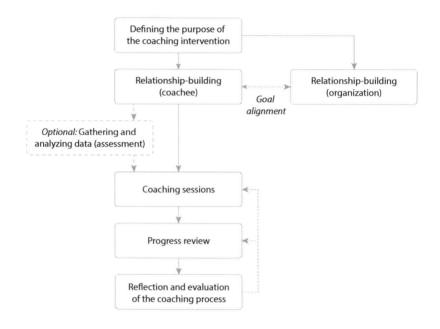

Figure 8 Typical phases of a coaching process

Defining the purpose of the coaching intervention

At the beginning of a new coaching relationship, it is always advisable to clearly define its purpose. When the purpose of coaching is clearly defined, both the coach and coachee can decide on whether coaching is really the right developmental intervention, and whether the coach is really the right person for that purpose.

Regardless of the setting, the coach and coachee need to answer the following questions to **clarify the purpose of coaching** before the actual coaching intervention begins:[1]

- **What is the topic or issue that the coachee wants to explore?** Is the coachee dissatisfied with the current situation? Which problem needs to be solved? Why is that important for the coachee? What would the coachee like to achieve and why? How can the coaching intervention contribute to achieving the coachee's goals? Is it possible to set criteria for an appropriate resolution of the issue up-front?

- **Who are the key stakeholders and what are their expectations?** Who else is interested in—or can influence—the definition and outcome of the coaching intervention (e.g. the coachee's manager, the human resource manager of the organization, or another sponsor)? What are the objectives of these stakeholders? What outcomes or results do they expect from the coaching intervention?
- **What are the roles of the coach, the coachee, and key stakeholders?** What does the coachee expect from the coach? What does the coach expect from the coachee? How do the coach and coachee see their roles (e.g. the coach's role as a facilitator rather than an advisor)? What are the boundaries of the coaching work (what cannot be done)? In what form must key stakeholders be included during the coaching process?
- **How is the coaching intervention linked to the wider organizational context?** In what way is the coaching relationship important for the organization? What other factors in the organizational context could contribute to—or form an obstacle to—the success of the coaching intervention?

Reaching a shared understanding of the purpose and goal of a coaching intervention is an important precondition for its effectiveness. Another important step in preparing an effective coaching relationship is to form a common understanding of the nature of coaching—so that the coachee does not expect to get consultancy or counseling instead of coaching.

The purpose of the coaching intervention is usually defined at an **introductory meeting** which is not yet a coaching conversation. In some introductory meetings, the coach will also meet a representative of the client organization (e.g. the coachee's direct manager or a human resource manager) in addition to the coachee.

Other points that are usually discussed in an introductory meeting include:

- relevant background information about the coach and coachee,
- a presentation of the coaching approach, and
- logistical issues (when and where the coaching will take place).[2]

THE PURPOSE AND CONTEXT OF A COACHING INTERVENTION

Step 1: Find a learning partner (e.g. a fellow coaching student or a trusted colleague or friend). Ask them to think about an issue that they would like to be coached on.

Step 2: Use the questions from this section of the book to clearly define the purpose of a potential coaching intervention for the issue that your partner raises. Use the following form as a guideline for capturing all the relevant information.

Topic/issue to be explored	

Key stakeholders	Expectation of stakeholders

Coach's role	
Coachee's expectations of the coach	
Coachee's role	
Coach's expectations of the coachee	

Relevant contextual factors	Implications for the coaching process

Purpose statement: *"The purpose of the coaching intervention is to ..."*	

The physical space in which coaching takes place can have an effect on its effectiveness. Finding a quiet space without distractions is a precondition for holding a deep and focused conversation. This does not necessarily have to be an office or a meeting room. It is possible to hold a good coaching conversation, for example, during a walk in the countryside.[3]

Building the relationship with the organization

For external executive coaches, it is particularly important to reach a clear agreement with the sponsoring organization about the **goals of a coaching assignment**.

Ideally, the goal for the coaching assignment is not defined too narrowly. In a *Harvard Business Review* survey of 140 executive coaches, more than 90 percent reported that the focus of their coaching engagements sometimes shifts from the original intention.[4]

Nevertheless, it is good practice to create a **contract with the sponsoring organization** that clearly includes the expectations and responsibilities of all parties (the coach, the coachee, and the organization).

Such a contract could, for example, include:

- The purpose or goal of the coaching intervention (desired outcomes)
- The intended number and duration of coaching sessions
- The duration of the coaching service
- The compensation for the coach (fees, expenses, terms of payment)
- The coaching setting (face-to-face/location, videoconference, email, or telephone)
- The potential use of assessment and testing tools (e.g. personality profiles) and the cost that might be incurred for using these tools
- Any support that is required by the organization
- A confidentiality clause

At the beginning of the coaching process, coaches should also familiarize themselves with the **organizational context**—including the organizational culture, the goals of the organization and its top managers, relevant formal structures and processes, and particularly any informal power relationships that could have an effect on the coachee's effectiveness at work. Some human resource managers explicitly require such a familiarization process when they start working with a new external executive coach.[5]

An executive coach will then typically try to find out how the representatives of the sponsoring organization see the link between the coaching assignment and their organizational goals.

The triangular relationship between the coach, the coachee, and the client organization inherently includes the potential for conflict, especially regarding loyalty and confidentiality. Ensuring **alignment between the organization's and the coachee's goals** early on is important to avoid goal conflicts later in the coaching relationship.

Sponsors in the organization will usually want to be informed about the **progress and results of the coaching intervention**. One way to keep sponsors informed is to arrange feedback meetings between the coachee and their sponsor in the organization. If the sponsor would like to get feedback directly from the coach, it is advisable that the coach discusses the main points that they will inform the sponsor about with the coachee first. Otherwise, they risk a breach of trust in their relationship with the coachee.

Building the relationship with the coachee

As we saw in Chapter 1, many studies confirm that the **quality of the relationship** between the coach and coachee is a key factor in determining whether a coaching engagement will succeed.[6]

At the beginning of a new coaching relationship, coachees will often ask themselves whether the coach is really the right person to support them on their development path. They will usually want to know more about the **qualifications and experience of the coach**. An external coach can help new coachees with their 'credibility assessment'[7] through, for example, providing their CV up-front or sharing relevant information about their background, certifications, and prior success stories.

Right from the beginning, coachees will also assess a coach's knowledge and self-confidence, and whether they like their **coaching style**.[8] How closely a coach's style matches the coachee's preferred style matters when it comes to, for example, assertiveness, performance orientation, and the extent to which they like to follow a structured process or have a more open and flexible discussion. As in other relationships, the right 'chemistry' between the coach and coachee is important.

One of the main characteristics of a good relationship between a coach and coachee is a **high level of trust**. Several researchers have examined which actions can foster interpersonal trust. These actions send 'positive relational signals'—they make the coachee feel that the coach really cares for their well-being.[9]

Such **trust-building actions** include, for example:[10]

- **Being open and honest**—sharing valuable information, giving positive and constructive feedback, and being honest about one's own motives.
- **Ensuring confidentiality**—it is important for a coach to discuss any concerns about confidentiality with the coachee at the beginning of the coaching process.
- **Managing mutual expectations**—discussing the expectations of both sides at the beginning of the coaching relationship, and regularly reviewing the effectiveness of the collaboration.
- **Keeping commitments**—if a coach promises to do something by a certain date, they should make sure they definitely do it.
- **Showing care and concern for the coachee and their interests**—always remaining focused on the goals of the coachee, and supporting them in making progress.
- **Bolstering the self-confidence of the coachee**—encouraging and complimenting them in coaching conversations, and speaking positively about them in public settings.

In order for coaching to be effective, coachees must also feel that they are in a safe environment where privacy and confidentiality are assured, and that the coach is treating them in a non-judgmental and supportive way.[11]

Gathering and analyzing data

Some executive coaching relationships begin with an **assessment phase** in which the coach gathers data about the four **GAPS factors**:[12]

- Goals and values of the coachee
- Abilities and strengths of the coachee
- Perceptions of others about the coachee
- Success factors—what the coachee needs to perform well in their organizational role (in terms of attitudes, behaviors, relationships, and results)

Tools for assessing the GAPS factors can include:

- Questionnaire-based analyses of the coachee's values (also known as 'values inventories') and interests, and exercises in which coachees reflect on their values and goals (for 'G' in GAPS).
- Personality inventories, ability tests, and strengths-finding question-naires (for 'A').
- 360-degree feedback surveys (in which feedback is gathered from the coachee's subordinates, peers, and supervisors) or interviews with people who know the coachee well (for 'P').
- Expectations of stakeholders (based on interviews with them), job descriptions, or competency profiles (for 'S').

The coach would then analyze the data together with the coachee to **iden-tify strengths and development needs.**

The primary purpose of the data gathering and analysis stage is to help the coachee **develop insight**—to "understand what areas they need to develop to be more effective."[13] The coach and coachee can then use the results of the analysis as an input for setting an agenda (with specific development or behavior change goals) for the coaching intervention.

COACHING BEST PRACTICE

WORKING WITH A 'DISCOVERY QUESTIONNAIRE'

Steve Schlafman (also widely known as 'Schlaf') is a New York-based pro-fessional certified coach who is specialized in coaching entrepreneurs and "leaders in transition."

He prefers to refer to his coachees as "coaching partners" rather than "clients" and views the work with his coachees as "co-creation." "I seek to build and cultivate a symbiotic relationship where we grow, learn, and thrive together," is how he explains his approach to prospective coachees. "Our partnership is built on a foundation of trust, mutual respect, collabo-ration, and growth."

Schlafman usually kicks off the relationship with his new coaching partners in what he calls a Discovery Session. In this 90-minutes session, he tries to clarify mutual expectations and intentions for the coaching relationship, agree on logistical issues, address any questions that the coachee might have, and discuss the results of a Discovery Questionnaire which he sends out to his coachees before the session.

The Discovery Questionnaire is designed to help the coachees think about who they are as a leader and human: "This includes your values, habits, strengths, blockers, goals, and much more," explains Schlafman. "The questionnaire also helps you clearly define what you want achieve together in the first 3–6 months. We review this document every few months to see how you're changing and progressing towards the future you envision."

The Discovery Questionnaire helps coachees to better understand themselves. It is also a tool for both partners to more clearly define and keep track of the main intentions and goals of the coaching relationship.

Source: https://schlaf.me/howitworks/ (accessed 1 February 2021). With kind permission of Steve Schlafman.

Coaching sessions

Most of the coaching work takes place in **coaching sessions.** In these sessions, the coach helps the coachee:

- express *where they want to be* (their goals),
- understand *where they are now* (the current situation including relevant relationships, the coachee's own thoughts and habits, and constraints), and
- find the *right way to reach their goals* (through exploring different options and committing to a concrete action plan).

Coaching sessions typically follow a **structure** that looks similar to the following (see Figure 9):

1. **Reconnecting.** Making sure the coachee is fully present for the coaching meeting—two or three sentences of small talk can help the coachee to feel at ease and make the transition from whatever they were doing before to fully focusing on the coaching conversation.

2. **Progress review (follow-up).** Jointly reviewing the coachee's actions between the sessions (based on the agreements from the previous coaching session) and reflecting on outcomes and learnings.
3. **Setting the agenda.** Choosing the topic and setting clear goals for the current session, and defining any outcomes that the coachee wants to achieve.
4. **The goal-oriented coaching conversation.** Exploring the focus topic of the session and helping the coachee to develop options and create a concrete action plan (e.g. following the GROW model—see Chapter 2).
5. **Setting up accountability.** Summarizing the main points of the discussion and agreeing on next action steps (what the coachee will do, by when).

Figure 9 Typical structure of a coaching session

To be able to follow a structured coaching process, coaches usually **take notes** during the coaching sessions. Writing down the main points and key phrases can free the coach up from needing to remember everything. Thus, they can better manage the process and focus on what the coachee has to say.

Going through notes from previous sessions before a new coaching session begins can also help the coach reflect on their coachee's goals and their own contribution to reaching these goals.[14]

Progress review (follow-up)

At the beginning of a new coaching session, the coach and coachee will usually take a look at to what extent the coachee has implemented the goal-oriented actions that were agreed at the end of the previous session.

The coach's role here is not to supervise or check up on the coachee, but to act as an **accountability partner** and to **facilitate the coachee's learning process.**[15]

Coaches can also use the follow-up part of a coaching conversation for **recognizing progress and success** (for example, by saying *"It is great to hear that your actions had such a positive outcome—congratulations!"*). This can have a positive effect on both the motivation and self-confidence of the coachee.

Reviewing the coachee's action plan is one way to create accountability. Examples of other techniques that can also foster accountability include a **daily journal**, in which a coachee records certain behaviors, or regular **feedback and review meetings** between the coachee and their boss.[16]

COACHING QUESTIONS

COACHING QUESTIONS FOR A PROGESS REVIEW (FOLLOW-UP)

Here are some questions that coaches can use to explore the progress that their coachees have made between coaching sessions:

- "Which actions did you take?"
- "What was the impact of your actions?"
- "To what extent did you achieve your goal?"
- "What worked particularly well (and why)?"
- "Which of your actions were particularly effective?"

- "What could have gone better?"
- "What surprised you about what happened?"
- "Were there any of the agreed actions that you did not take? What were your reasons for deciding not to take these actions?"
- "How did your views about the situation change?"
- "How do you feel about your progress?"

Effective follow-up questions also focus on facilitating the coachee's learning process. Consider the following examples:

- "What do learn from this?"
- "What is the most useful insight for you?"
- "What is the one thing that you would like to remember?"
- "How will you use your learnings in future?"
- "What will you do next time you face a similar challenge?"
- "What will you do differently next time?"
- "What do you want to develop further as a consequence?"

THE WEEKLY ACCOUNTABILITY EMAIL

Mo Chanmugham is a former entertainment lawyer who became a certified executive coach. To help his clients "keep their momentum going in between sessions," Chanmugham has integrated a weekly accountability email into his coaching service.

"While the coaching sessions are designed to help clients get clarity and get unstuck, the real work happens in between sessions," he says. "That is when they have to go out in the world and actually do what they said they were going to do."

That is why every Monday, he sends out a "gentle reminder to stay focused on their goals and to ask for help if they feel stuck." The accountability email includes the following three questions:

- *"What is your number one goal this week and when will it be done by?"* (Goal)
- *"What are you struggling with and what will you do to address this? Also, how can I support you?"* (Challenge)
- *"Optional, feel free to share any wins, lessons learned, and/or questions you have."* (Win)

He also includes himself in the process and shares his own goals, challenges, and wins of the week with his coachees, too.

Chanmugham believes that public accountability is one of the most effective ways of getting things done, as no one likes to look bad in front of others. What is more, he says, "it is only by sharing what keeps us stuck, that we can get unstuck." Through providing his coachees with an opportunity to share their struggles and challenges, he also helps them to escape patterns of avoidance and procrastination.

Source: http://www.mgccoaching.com/blog/2019/12/16/the-power-of-a-weekly-accountability-email-to-help-you-reach-your-goals (accessed 1 February 2021). With kind permission of Mo Chanmugham.

Reflection and evaluation of the coaching process

Regular reflection on the coaching process can help to ensure its effectiveness. This can be done more informally, for example as a **'quick check' reflection** at the end of a coaching session, or in a more formal way as a scheduled 'interim balance' or final **evaluation meeting**.

In both settings, formal or informal, the following questions can help the coach and coachee to jointly **reflect on the effectiveness of the coaching process**. The coach could ask the coachee:

- To what degree have we achieved the initial goals of the coaching assignment?
- How did you progress in your development during our coaching relationship?
- Is the coaching intervention effective in addressing your development needs?
- What did you learn about yourself in the coaching relationship?
- How do you see things differently now?

- Which influence did the coaching relationship have on your actions?
- How effective are the coaching sessions?
- What works particularly well in the coaching relationship?
- What do you find useful about our discussions? Is there anything that you find less useful?
- Is there anything that I could do differently to support you more effectively?
- What could we do to further improve the coaching sessions?

In addition to the feedback they get from their coachees, coaches can also make their **own regular reflection and progress reviews** with the help of their notes.[17] Self-reflection questions could, for example, include: *"What can I learn from this conversation?"*, *"What worked well in the conversation?"*, or *"What could I do differently next time?"*

Some coaches also work with **coaching supervisors** to reflect on their professional practice. These are professionals who help coaches further develop their coaching skills (the *developmental function* of the supervisor), provide them with a 'safe space' to talk about the conversations and experiences they are having with their clients (*resourcing function*), and ensure the quality and integrity of their work (*qualitative function*).[18]

As the coach acts as a learning, development, and accountability partner for a coachee, so does the supervisor for a coach.

KEEP A REFLECTIVE DIARY

A reflective diary (also known as a reflective journal)—no matter whether it is paper-based or in electronic form—can be a powerful learning and development tool for coaches.

After each coaching session, take a few minutes to go through your notes again. Write down your most important learnings from the session in your diary.

You can use the following questions to guide your reflection process:

- How do I feel about the interaction with the coachee? Why do I feel this way?
- What worked particularly well in this session (and why)?
- What was less effective (and why)?
- Did I forget something in this conversation?
- Was there a critical incident/a particularly difficult situation during the conversation? Is there anything that I could have said or done differently in that situation?
- Did I have the right mindset in this conversation? Do I need to change anything in my attitude?
- What is the most important learning for me from this coaching conversation?
- What will I do differently next time?

EFFECTIVE COACHING CONVERSATIONS: A BRIEF SUMMARY IN 10 POINTS

1. A **professional coaching process** includes several phases: defining the purpose of the coaching intervention, building the relationship with the organization and coachee, gathering and analyzing data (optional), coaching sessions, progress reviews, and the reflection and evaluation of the coaching process.

2. A clear **agreement on the purpose of the coaching intervention** between the coach, the coachee, and the client organization is an essential starting point for every professional coaching relationship.

3. Executive coaches need to build a formal (contractual) **relationship with the client organization** and should also familiarize themselves with the organizational context.

4. The quality of the **relationship between the coach and coachee** is a key success factor for coaching.

5. Coaches need to **build trust** with the coachee, e.g. through ensuring confidentiality, keeping commitments, creating a safe environment for the coachee, and showing concern for the coachee and their interests.

6. Some coaching relationships include an **assessment phase**, in which the coach first collects data about the coachee (e.g. by using questionnaires or gathering feedback from others). The coach and coachee then analyze the assessment data with the aim of developing additional insights.

7. Assessments typically include the four **GAPS factors**: **g**oals and values, **a**bilities and strengths, **p**erceptions that others have about the coachee, and **s**uccess factors for performing well in the coachee's organizational role.

8. **Coaching sessions** are the core of the coaching process. They typically include the following parts: reconnecting, progress review, setting the agenda, the goal-oriented coaching conversation, and setting up accountability.

9. **Progress reviews** are useful to ensure accountability, enhance the coachee's motivation, and recognize and celebrate progress.

10. Regular **joint reflection** of the coaching process can help to ensure its effectiveness.

Notes for Chapter 3

1   Lane & Corrie (2021).
2   Starr (2016).
3   Starr (2016).
4   Kauffman & Coutu (2008).
5   Fillery-Travis & Lane (2021).
6   Passmore & Fillery-Travis (2011).
7   Natale & Diamante (2005), p. 364.
8   Natale & Diamante (2005).
9   Six (2005), p. 82.
10 Six et al. (2010); Starr (2016).
11 Rekalde et al. (2017).
12 Peterson (2011).
13 Peterson (2011), p. 539.
14 Starr (2016), p. 27.
15 Whitmore (2017).
16 Peterson (2011).
17 Starr (2016).
18 Hawkins & Smith (2013).

ESSENTIAL COACHING SKILLS

··

This chapter will enable you to

» Develop the mindset needed to become an effective coach.
» Formulate coaching questions that will help coachees make progress on issues that are important to them.
» Enhance your active listening skills.
» Give constructive feedback to coachees.
» Help you and your coachee deal with difficult emotional situations.

··

There is a certain skillset that every effective coach needs to master. Coaching mainly takes place in the form of conversations in which coaches use a questioning approach to support their coachees. **Questioning and active listening skills** are therefore of utmost importance for any coach.

Further essential conversational skills include the ability to **summarize** parts of the coaching discussion in a goal-oriented way and to **provide constructive feedback** to coachees.

Many of the topics discussed in coaching sessions are emotionally charged. Coaches therefore also need **emotional intelligence**—the ability to understand and positively deal with both their own emotions and the emotions of others—as well as an ability to help their coachees **develop awareness of the emotional state of others**.

In this chapter, we will explore these key coaching skills in more detail. But let us first start with a fundamental coaching skill—forming a **coaching mindset**.

The coaching mindset

For coaching to be effective, coaches need to develop a positive coaching mindset (see Figure 10). This typically includes:

- **A collaborative attitude** instead of a directive approach. The coach is not the coachee's boss or teacher. Coaching is a partnership of equals. Even if the coach thinks they have good advice to share, it is good practice to ask the coachee for permission first (e.g. *"Would you like me to add something out of my own experience here?"* or *"May I share an observation with you?"*).

- **A supportive attitude**. Coachees must feel that the coach really wants to help them. This includes taking a neutral stance and suspending judgment of the coachee's behavior. It is not the job of the coach to tell the coachee what is 'right' or 'wrong' about their behavior. A coach's job is to help the coachee find the solutions and actions that are the right ones from their own perspective.

- **A clear focus on the coachee**. Trained coaches typically do not make suggestions for what they would do if they were in the coachee's shoes. A coach is not supposed to solve the coachee's problems for them. Instead, coaching is about "working with someone to help them get where they want to go."[1]

- **Belief in the coachee's potential**. Effective coaches do not think that coachees 'have a problem,' or even worse that they 'are a problem.' Instead, they recognize that their coachees are on a learning journey on which they have not yet realized their full potential.[2] You cannot coach someone if you do not believe in the other person's development potential.

- **Create "a forward-looking cognitive state in coachees."[3]** Coaching is about helping others to make progress toward the future, not about getting stuck in the problems of the past. This means that coaches must have a positive future- and solution-oriented mindset—a mindset that they ideally convey to their coachees.

For the coach, having a positive mindset is fundamental for a well-functioning coaching relationship. After all, coaching is about making a positive difference in the lives of others.

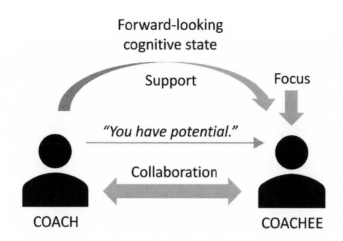

Forward-looking
cognitive state

Support   Focus

"You have potential."

Collaboration

COACH   COACHEE

Figure 10 The coaching mindset

COACHING BEST PRACTICE

GUIDING PRINCIPLES FOR YOUR COACHING PRACTICE

Some coaches make their coaching mindset explicit through establishing guiding principles for their own coaching practice.

As one example, here are the coaching principles of Pamela Fay, an executive coach and coaching supervisor from Ireland:

- *"Coaching is about supporting change and action.*
- *Coaching focuses on the client's story, thinking and feelings.*
- *The client sets the agenda for the coaching relationship and for each coaching session.*
- *Clients are resourceful and my role is to help them tap into their gut instinct and explore their options.*
- *Client and coach are equals in the coaching relationship.*
- *It is important for me to understand clients in the context of their organizational system."*

Source: https://www.pamelafay.ie (accessed 15 January 2021). With kind permission of Pamela Fay.

Questioning skills

"Tell less and ask more"[4]—this is the main advice that Michael Bungay Stanier (author of *The Coaching Habit*, one of the most successful books on coaching) gives to aspiring coaches. **Formulating the right questions** is one the most fundamental coaching skills.

Effective coaching questions are:

- simple and easy to understand,
- focused on bringing information to the surface and generating options that will help the coachee to make progress on the issues that are important to them,
- thought-provoking, and
- free of (implicit) advice, blame, or judgment.[5]

Powerful coaching questions focus the attention of the coachee on observing both the external and their internal reality, on finding solutions, and on committing to taking actions to improve their life.

It is important to **ask only one question at a time**. If a coach asks three questions in a row, it is difficult for a coachee to keep their mind focused, which is a major condition for making progress in their thinking process.

The main questioning technique that coaches use are **open-ended questions** that start with *"what," "how," "who," "when,"* or *"where."* Scenario-based questions can also sometimes be useful (e.g. *"If XY happened, what would you do?"*), especially for imagining an 'ideal' future state. Open-ended questions usually make people think. In exceptional cases, closed questions can also help to clarify certain issues (e.g. *"Did I understand that correctly?"*) or move the conversation forward (e.g. *"Would it be OK for you if we now take a look at the options that you have for dealing with this situation?"*).

One framework that can be used for helping coachees to **explore a situation with open questions** is the **TED model** (TED stands for 'tell,' 'example,' 'describe').[6] Here are a few examples of questions that follow the TED model:

- *"Could you tell me more about ...?"* (T)
- *"Could you give me an example for ...?"* (E)
- *"Could you describe this situation in a bit more detail?"* (D)[7]

Many experienced coaches suggest **avoiding 'why' questions**, as they could unnecessarily put the coachee in a defensive mode (they might think that they need to justify themselves). Instead of *"Why did you do that?"* a coach could, for example, ask *"What intention did you have with that?"* which could elicit the same kind of information, but in a less accusatory way.[8]

Coaches should generally **avoid leading questions** in which they include hidden but unsolicited advice (for example, *"Have you already considered ..."* or *"Have you thought of doing it in the following way: ...?"*).[9]

The table below provides some **examples of effective coaching questions** proposed by experienced coaches.

Coaching question	Purpose of the question
"What is the real challenge here for you?"[10]	This question provides the opportunity to dig deeper and uncover the 'real problem' (the root cause rather than the symptom). This question can also help a coachee to focus on the most important issue once they have identified different aspects that make a situation difficult for them. Note that the two words "for you" are a key element of the question, as they put the focus fully on the coachee.
"What do you really want?"[11]	Similar to the question above, this question tries to get to a deeper level. The aim of this question is to identify the real motivations behind the first goal that a coachee comes up with.
"If the meeting [or any other future situation] were wildly to exceed your expectations, what would happen in it?"[12] *"If the situation were perfect, what would it look like?"*[13]	With questions like these, the coach can try to help the coachee overcome limiting beliefs and find new ways of thinking about an ideal outcome. This can create positive energy while at the same time widening the potential solutions space.
"What is standing in your way?" *"If this obstacle did not exist, what would your life look like?"* *"So what can you do to overcome the obstacle?"*[14]	These questions help coachees clearly identify their 'roadblocks,' and at the same time evaluate whether they constitute real barriers. The third question directs a coachee's thoughts toward what they could do to remove or circumvent an obstacle.

Coaching question	Purpose of the question
"Can you tell me more?"[15] *"What else can you tell me about it?"*	Such follow-up questions may be asked several times in order to explore an issue in more depth (*"And what else is a challenge for you here?"*, *"Can you tell me more about what makes this so challenging for you?"*) or elicit additional options for dealing with an issue (*"And what else could you do about it?"*).
"With saying yes to this, what are you saying no to?"[16]	This question can help a coachee realize that solutions to particular problems are often linked to choosing what not to do. Whether it is about abandoning certain projects, breaking old habits, or saying no to some people—the 'what-not-to-do' part is often as important as the 'what-to-do' part when trying to make progress on resolving a certain issue.
"What conclusions are you drawing from that now?"[17]	This question can guide coachees toward summarizing their main insights and coming up with their own conclusions.
"What do you want to happen now?" *"What could you do to improve things now?"*[18]	These questions change the focus of the conversation from exploring what happened in the past to the present and future, and from being a passive observer to becoming an active 'doer.' Questions like these can be used for making the transition from the 'Reality' to the 'Options' phase in coaching conversations that follow the GROW model (see Chapter 2).
"I dont know where our conversation is heading—is this still a useful discussion?"[19]	Coaches can use this question if they feel that the discussion has digressed too far from the main issue, or when the conversation has reached a 'dead end.'

Another key skill for coaches is the ability to **translate problem statements into forward-looking and solution-oriented questions.**

Take, for example, the following problem statement: *"I can't find time for working on this really important project because I am drowning in day to day tasks."* Here is a translation of the problem statement into a solution-oriented question: *"How many hours per week do you need to work on your important project? What could you stop doing in order to make room for your important project?"*

Such questions can be very powerful if a coach formulates them in a way that (a) assumes there actually is an answer to the problem, (b) triggers a focused problem-solving process, and (c) is open enough to generate several creative solutions for the issue at hand.[20]

TRANSLATE A PROBLEM STATEMENT INTO SOLUTION-ORIENTED QUESTIONS

Step 1: Think about one issue or problem that you currently have yourself, or ask a learning partner to share an issue or problem with you. Take a piece of paper and write the problem statement down, beginning with: *"The problem is that ..."*

Step 2: Write down three to five different forward-looking and solution-oriented questions that you could ask yourself (or your learning partner) in order to start a constructive problem-solving process. Do not include advice or solutions in the questions (either explicitly or implicitly). Keep the questions open-ended but focused on triggering thought processes that will help you (or your learning partner) explore different options for solving the problem.

Active listening skills

Good coaches ask good questions—and then listen carefully to the coachee's answers.

If coaches do not listen well, they will not be able to really understand the coachee's situation, which means they cannot fully support them in making progress.

In everyday life, we often pretend to listen while thinking about our own answers and ideas instead. The other person will then usually notice that you are not fully 'with them.'

Coaching requires a deeper form of listening that is often referred to as 'active,' 'focused,' or 'attentive' listening.

In an **active listening mode**, coaches:

- **pay undivided attention** and show the coachee that they are fully involved (e.g. by nodding or using facial expressions that show interest in the coachee),
- **acknowledge what the coachee said and use paraphrasing and summarizing** to clarify and confirm that they correctly understood what was said (without conveying any judgment about it), and
- **ask additional clarifying questions** to encourage the coachee to tell them more about what they think and feel.[21]

When coaches listen actively, they do not only listen for what is said, but also for what remains unsaid. Underlying emotions, in particular, are sometimes more strongly conveyed through non-verbal signals. Listening 'between the lines' could, for example, include noticing the reluctance to directly answer a question, changes in the coachee's tone of voice, pauses in which the coachee remains silent, or signs in the coachee's body language that might offer additional clues about their feelings.

Note-taking is another tool that coaches use to convey to coachees that they are actively involved and really trying to understand what they say.

There are also some **things you don't do when you are in an active listening mode**. Ideally, you do not:

- attend to your own thoughts and ideas while the other person speaks,
- interrupt the speaker,
- finish their sentences (maybe incorrectly assuming that you already know what they want to tell you), and
- present your own views and opinions about the issue that you are discussing (instead you should suspend judgment).

This is not easy, as most of us have a natural tendency to share our thoughts when something that another person says triggers associations in our own mind. Coaches therefore need to consciously practice their active listening skills. As Sir John Whitmore succinctly put it: "Perhaps the hardest thing a coach has to learn is to shut up!"[22]

In short, in an active listening mode, the coach **focuses all of their attention on the coachee** with the clear aim of understanding what they really mean (see Figure 11).

ACTIVE LISTENING

👍 DO

Pay undivided attention ➡️

Acknowledge what was said ➡️

Paraphrase and summarize ➡️

Ask clarifying questions ➡️

DO NOT 👎

⬅️ Attend to your own thoughts

⬅️ Interrupt the speaker

⬅️ Finish sentences

⬅️ Present your own views

Figure 11 Active listening[36]

Summarizing skills

From time to time during a coaching session, coaches can provide a brief summary of part of the conversation—a concise overview of the main points that were just discussed.

Coachees can become tired of continually being asked questions. When the coach is summarizing, the coachee can get a short period of rest, in which they have time to reflect on what they have said.

Providing summaries—taking stock about 'where are we right now'—can have other positive effects too:[23]

- The coachee **feels that the coach has listened well** to what they have said and understands the situation correctly.
- It can help the coachee to **see the whole picture**.
- The coachee can also **refocus their attention on the goal** if the coach intelligently links the main points in their summary to the coachee's goal.
- The coachee might **form new links, associations, and insights** when they once again listen to what they have been saying.
- It provides a moment of pause that can be used as a **transition to a new part of the conversation**.

Summaries can be particularly helpful when either the coach or coachee is getting a bit lost or confused in the conversation, or when several different issues have been discussed, so that it is difficult for the discussion partners to keep them all in mind.[24]

Here are some examples of how a coach could start a summary:

- *"We have discussed quite a lot of different aspects regarding this issue now. May I try to summarize the main points?"*
- *"Did I get the three main points right? As far as I understood, these are ..."*
- *"Can I try to make a summary of what we have explored during the last 15 minutes?"*

As useful as they can be, using summaries too frequently can have a detrimental effect. They might put the focus of the discussion too much on the summarizing coach instead of on the coachee.

Remember that summarizing should not be confused with interpreting. Summaries report back to the coachee what the coach understood. They should not include the personal views and judgments of the coach.[25]

Constructive feedback skills

Feedback is a key ingredient of any learning process.

Before coachees can actively change something, they first need to be aware of what they actually need and want to change. "People's normal level of awareness is relatively low," observed coaching pioneer Sir John Whitmore.[26] Providing feedback is a particularly effective way of helping coachees to **raise their level of awareness**.

Feedback can be defined as **information that the coachee receives about their behavioral tendencies, actual behavior, and the effects of their behavior.**

A coachee can use this information to help make a change if they feel that this is necessary. Feedback should not, however, be confused with criticism. It is not the aim of feedback to express disapproval with something that the coachee does, but to provide them with additional input as a basis for their own development and decision-making processes.

Giving **constructive feedback**—information that might help the coachee achieve a positive outcome—is not always an easy task. People often react with negative emotions when they have the feeling that they are being criticized. It is therefore highly important how feedback is framed and conveyed.

Consider the following two statements:

1. *"You are not listening to me."*
2. *"I have the feeling that you are thinking about something here."*

Both statements can be used in the same situation. The first one might be seen as more aggressive, thus raising the chance of arousing negative feelings on the coachee's side. With the second statement, the coach conveys the information that they noticed the coachee was not listening, but in a more neutral tone and in a way that encourages further enquiry.

It is possible that sometimes, a coach feels that the coachee **needs to hear 'a tough message'**. In this case, a coach can consider the following points to ensure that the conversation still stays constructive and positive:[27]

- On balance, the conversation should stay on the positive side.
- Make clear that you are sharing personal observations (*"I have the feeling …"*, *"I feel …"*, *"I noticed that …"*) instead of uncontestable facts (*"You are …"*, *"You do not …"*).
- Avoid negatively loaded words that could make the coachee feel uncomfortable (instead of *"I think you are a whiner,"* you might also say *"I notice that you are often expressing disappointment about your fellow team members."*).
- Use positive non-verbal signals (e.g. a positive tone of voice, eye contact).
- Use open questions to let the coachee voice their own opinion and thoughts about the issue (*"What is your view on this?"*).
- Try to link your observations to the coachee's goal (e.g. *"I noticed that you struggled to meet the deadline for this task. As one of your main goals is to complete the whole project in time, what could you do to ensure that you will finish on time with your next tasks?"*).

There are two basic goals that coaches should keep in mind when giving constructive feedback: first, to convey information to the coachee in a way that helps them raise their self-awareness, and second, to help the coachee maintain a positive emotional state.[28]

SHARING CONSTRUCTIVE FEEDBACK

Step 1: Find one person to whom you could provide constructive feedback. Prepare your feedback conversation in advance. Write down the answers to the following questions:

- What information would you like to convey to the recipient of the feedback?
- What will you tell the person? What will you ask them?
- How will you ensure that the feedback is seen as non-judgmental and constructive?
- How will you ensure that the recipient maintains a positive emotional state?
- Which reactions do you expect from the recipient of the feedback?

Step 2: Hold the feedback conversation. Pay close attention to both verbal and non-verbal reactions of the recipient. If possible, ask the recipient what they think about how you conveyed the feedback, and what could have been more effective.

Step 3: Reflect on your learnings from the feedback conversation:

- How did the recipient react to your feedback (and how did this differ from your expectations)?
- What worked well in the feedback conversation? What would you like to keep for further feedback conversations?
- What was challenging for you in the conversation? What would you do differently next time you hold a feedback conversation?

Helping coachees develop awareness of others

Coaching conversations often revolve around issues related to the relationships that coachees have with others. Coaches can help coachees to 'step into the shoes of others' and see the situation from another person's perspective. In doing so, they can support coachees in increasing their level of **social awareness**, which is a key ingredient of emotional intelligence.[29]

Here are a few questioning techniques that coaches can use to help coachees **develop or increase awareness of others**. They can ask the coachee to:

- explore how others think (*"What thoughts would Alex have about this?"*) or feel (*"How do you think Alex felt in this situation?"*),
- interpret the feelings of others (*"What makes you think she was angry about it?"*),
- understand the potential motivations of others (*"What are possible reasons for her to act in this way?"*, *"What do you think is the most important thing for her regarding this situation?"*),
- reflect on the perspective of others (*"If she were here with us now, what would she say about the situation?"*, *"Does she know how you feel about this?"*),
- predict how other people could react in a certain situation (*"If you told her about this, how might she react?"*).[30]

With a higher degree of social awareness, coachees will realize what effect their own actions have on other people. This can help them identify more sustainable solutions that others who are involved in the (relationship) issue are also more likely to accept and support.

Dealing with emotions

During a coaching conversation, a coachee might show strong emotions. This can also affect the emotional state of the coach, especially if the coachee's emotions are negative ones.

In general, "skilled coaches will not shy away from feeling states and will integrate emotion (and its impact on behavior) into the coaching process."[31] Emotions can be useful. After all, understanding the internal reality of coachees is an important building block in helping them to make progress on the issues that are important to them.

Coaches can **deal with the strong negative emotions of a coachee** in several ways:[32]

- Explore the emotion together with the client
- Take a time-out to be able to reflect on the emotion (without being in an emotional state themselves)
- Stop the coaching relationship and/or refer the coachee either to another coach or to a professional psychotherapist (if necessary)

When a person whom we have a good relationship with is really angry about a situation, we often tend to sympathize (*"Yes, you are absolutely right. I would also feel bad about this"*). A sympathetic response might be appropriate in certain circumstances, but often **sympathizing can make a coach too emotionally involved**. It can also potentially strengthen the coachee's belief that they are a 'victim.'

An alternative way of dealing with such a situation is to first acknowledge the feelings of the coachee, but then to try to progress with the conversation in a goal-oriented way (e.g. *"Yes, I can understand why you are angry about that. Let us explore together what led to this situation."*).[33]

A coach can help a coachee to **get out of a 'victim mindset.'** When the coachee feels that something bad happened to them, when they blame other people, or when they complain about all the things that are going wrong, it is probably time to shift the focus of the conversation. Coaches could, for example, try to focus on potential solutions and steps that the coachee could actively take to make progress.

When a person encounters a difficult situation, they can think of it in terms of *"I am in deep trouble here"* or slightly differently, in terms of *"What can I do to improve this admittedly very difficult situation?"* They could say *"There is nothing I can do about it"* or alternatively *"The current circumstances are limiting my options. Is there anything I can do to change the circumstances?"*

You can easily spot the difference here. It is a difference in attitude. The former statements are examples of the 'victim mode,' the latter ones of an attitude of being a **pilot of your own life**.

According to the British executive coaches Joseph O'Connor and Andrea Lages, it is one of the main roles of a coach to help their coachees "to be more of a creator of their life."[34] While victims feel that they are "at the mercy of outside events," creators (or pilots) know that even when they cannot change events, they can at least choose how to think about and react to these events.

"A creator sees the outside world as feedback; a victim sees it as coercion,"[35] write O'Connor and Lages. Good coaches want to see their coachees in the creator mode.

HELPING COACHEES MANAGE THEIR EMOTIONS

Sue Belton is a former BBC journalist and executive life coach based in London, England. In her coaching practice, she often works with clients who experience strong negative work-related emotions like anger, anxiety, or sadness.

Belton uses what she calls an **'AAA exercise'** to help her clients manage their emotions, either directly in the moment in which an emotion arises (after taking a few deep breaths), or later as a means of reflection.

Step 1 of the exercise (**'Accept'**) is to identify and accept the emotion: "As soon as you are aware of this emotion, as soon as you feel it in your body (e.g. the burning/tightness of anger), take a moment and accept it," recommends Belton. "You can even state (internally or externally) 'I feel angry' or 'I feel sad'. The key here is not to try and escape from it or push it away—this is what often happens, and that is why the pause is helpful here. Identify the emotion."

Step 2 (**'Allow'**) is about allowing yourself to feel the emotion. Belton's advice is to let the emotion "run through your body" and to "go to where it is in your body." When you have closely observed what is happening in your body, you can take a deep breath again. "It is the act of going there and staying there (versus avoidance or suppression) that is important," says Belton. "When you have done this successfully, you will ultimately feel that shift, that dissipation, that sense of calm."

The final step (**'Ask'**) is a deeper exploration of what the emotion actually means:

- "What is this emotion telling me? What is the message?"
- "What is one thing I can do about this situation?"
- "What is the one thing I need to accept this situation?"

Through following the AAA process, coachees can become more conscious about their emotions and develop a better understanding of the messages that they convey. "And in doing so," says Belton, they are also prepared to "choose another way to feel and respond."

Source: https://suebelton.com/how-manage-emotions-at-work/ (accessed 4 February 2021). With kind permission of Sue Belton.

ESSENTIAL COACHING SKILLS: A BRIEF SUMMARY IN 10 POINTS

1. Effective coaches approach the coaching task with a **positive mindset**.

2. A **'coaching mindset'** includes a collaborative and supportive attitude, belief in the potential of the coachee, and a commitment to developing a forward-looking state of mind in the coachee.

3. **Questioning skills** are extremely important for coaches. Effective coaching questions are easy to understand, non-judgmental, and focused on making progress on the issues that are important for the coachee.

4. Coaching requires a deeper form of listening (known as **'active listening'**) in which a coach pays undivided attention to the coachee, acknowledges and paraphrases what the coachee says, and asks clarifying questions.

5. Active listeners do not only listen for what is being said, but also for **what remains unsaid**.

6. Coaches can provide **summaries** to structure a conversation and enable the coachee to see the whole picture and form new insights.

7. **Constructive feedback** can help a coachee raise their level of self-awareness. Such feedback conveys information about the coachee in a non-judgmental and neutral tone, and in a way that fosters further enquiry and development.

8. Coaches should try to help their coachees maintain a **positive emotional state**.

9. Several techniques can be used to help a coachee **develop awareness of others** (e.g. exploring what others think, interpreting their feelings, reflecting on the motivations and perspectives of others, and predicting how others could react in a certain situation).

10. Coaches need to expect and deal with **a coachee's negative emotions**. Sympathizing is usually not the right approach here, as it fosters a 'victim mindset.' Acknowledging the coachee's feelings and then directing the focus toward what they can actively do to change things for the better (as 'pilots' or 'creators' of their own life) is a more effective approach for dealing with emotions.

Notes for Chapter 4

1 Starr (2016), p. 42.
2 Whitmore (2017), p. 61.
3 Lai & Palmer (2019), p. 158
4 Bungay Stanier (2016), p. 59.
5 Loehr (2008); Starr (2016).
6 O'Connor & Langes (2019).
7 O'Connor & Langes (2019).
8 Su (2014).
9 Bungay Stanier (2016), p. 73.
10 Bungay Stanier (2016), p. 84.
11 Whitmore (2017), p. 85.
12 Whitmore (2017), p. 63.
13 Cardon (2008).
14 All three questions from Forbes Coaches Council (2018).
15 Forbes Coaches Council (2018).
16 A very similar question was proposed by Bungay Stanier (2016), p. 163.
17 Starr (2016), p. 94.
18 Both questions from Starr (2016), p. 98.
19 Starr (2016), p. 100.
20 Starr (2016).
21 Weger Jr. et al. (2010).
22 Whitmore (2017), p. 90.
23 Starr (2016).
24 Open University (2016).
25 Open University (2016).
26 Whitmore (2017), p. 70.
27 Starr (2016).
28 Starr (2016).
29 Cherniss et al. (2006).
30 Starr (2016).
31 Natale & Diamante (2005), p. 366.
32 Cox & Bachkirova (2021).
33 O'Connor & Langes (2019), p. 33.
34 O'Connor & Langes (2019), p. 33.
35 Starr (2016).
36 Graphic representation by the author partly based on contents from Weger Jr. et al. (2010); source of ear graphic: openclipart.org.

COACHING TOOLS

This chapter will enable you to

» Select coaching tools that can help coachees better understand themselves.
» Apply coaching tools that can facilitate the behavior change of coachees.
» Support coachees in their goal-setting process.
» Reframe a problem in a way that opens up the space for new solutions.
» Use action memos to focus coachees on goal-oriented action.

Coaches do not solve problems for their coachees. Their task is to help coachees solve problems on their own. In order to make this possible, coaches use tools for structuring a goal-oriented thinking process (such as the GROW model or a cognitive behavioral coaching process model—see Chapter 2).

But there is also a wider set of coaching tools beyond the process models. Examples include:

- Tools for raising a coachee's **self-awareness**.
- **Motivational interviewing** as a tool for strengthening a coachee's motivation and commitment to change.
- The **transtheoretical model** as a tool for facilitating behavior change.
- **Goal-setting tools** that help a coachee identify and set their goals.

- Tools for **reframing** a problem.
- The **action memo** as a tool for keeping a coachee focused on their goals.

In this chapter we will take a closer look at each of these tools.

Tools for raising a coachee's self-awareness

There are several tools that coaches use to help coachees better understand themselves and their behavioral tendencies:

- **Personality profiles.** With the help of different questionnaire-based tools, coachees can explore their own personality types (the Myers-Briggs Type Indicator® test or the DiSC® profile are examples of widely used tests, but there are many other personality tests, too—some of them must be paid for, others are freely available on the internet). Personality traits can strongly influence behavioral tendencies. Making these traits explicit can help a coachee better assess their own strengths as well as potential blind spots. Research confirms that the use of personality assessment tools can improve coaching effectiveness.[1]
- **Strengths profiles.** Strengths assessment tools, for example Clifton-Strengths by Gallup® or the Cappfinity Strengths Profile, can help coachees to get better insights into which tasks they are likely to perform well in.
- **Team roles tests.** There are also tools for testing coachees' preferred roles in a team. The Belbin® test is a good example of this. Such tests can help coachees to understand how they can best contribute in team situations.
- **Feedback from others.** Many executive coaches see a 360-degree feedback as one of the most valuable tools in the coaching process.[2] '360-degree' means that the coachee gets feedback about their behavioral tendencies 'from all sides,' i.e. from peers, superiors, and people who report to them. Such feedback can help a coachee to get different perspectives on their behavior and performance. Coachees can either gather feedback directly from others, or they may ask the coach to conduct feedback interviews on their behalf.
- **Self-reflection exercises.** In a self-reflection exercise, coachees answer a set of questions (e.g. about their goals or key learnings) in written

form. As a special form of self-reflection, coachees can also keep a diary in which they regularly record their actions or observations regarding the issue they are being coached on.

- **Reading books**. Books about human behavior can help coachees reflect on their own behavioral tendencies. A coach could, for example, suggest that the coachee reads a certain book (or book chapters). In the following coaching session, the coach and coachee would then discuss how the content of the book relates to the coachee's own situation and goals.

EXERCISE

CONDUCTING A FEEDBACK INTERVIEW

Step 1: Ask a learning partner (your 'coachee') to nominate a person who could provide feedback about them. Let the learning partner organize the first contact with that person and arrange a 15 to 30 minute interview (either via telephone, videoconference, or face-to-face) in which you can ask the following questions:

- "What is [the coachee] really good at?"
- "Do you remember a situation in which [the coachee] performed exceptionally well? What do you think contributed to this exceptional performance?"
- "What did you learn from [the coachee]?"
- "What do you value most about [the coachee]?"
- "What could [the coachee] improve?"
- "What would [the coachee] need to do differently in order to become even more effective in their role?"
- "Do you have any other feedback for [the coachee]?"

Make sure to take proper notes during the interview.

Step 2: After the interview, get together with your learning partner again. Share the feedback that you received about them.

Ask your learning partner to reflect on the feedback. What do they learn from the feedback about themselves? Does the feedback confirm or contradict their own views about themselves? Is there anything that they would like to work on (e.g. setting a new development goal for themselves) as a result of the feedback?

Source: inspired by contents in Starr (2016).

Motivational interviewing

Motivational interviewing (MI) is a method that was originally developed by clinical therapists to help people overcome drug and alcohol addictions. It is based on the observation that clients who **communicate their motivation and commitment to change during a conversation** with their therapist have a much higher chance of successfully changing their behaviors.[3]

People do not change because they are *told* to change. They do so because they want to change. The aim of MI is to help people express their wish to change and uncover their deeper motivations for change. As MI pioneers Miller and Rollnick succinctly summarized: "People talk *themselves* into changing."[4]

MI can also be applied in coaching, especially when the goal of the coaching intervention is to help a coachee overcome an unhelpful behavioral tendency.

The basic idea behind MI is to have a conversation about change—**a conversation that strengthens the coachee's motivation and commitment to change**.[5]

Based on the precondition of having set up a trusting working relationship between the coach and coachee, three steps are typically involved in the MI process:[6]

1. **Focusing**—clarifying the change goals (*"What do I want to change?"*)
2. **Evoking**—helping the coachee uncover and clearly voice their own motivations for change; this is the 'heart' of the MI process (*"Why do I want to change?"*)

3. **Planning**—helping the coachee commit to certain action steps that will enable them to change (*"What steps will I take to change [and when]? How will I stay committed?"*)

During MI, the coach should always keep the main aims of the conversation in mind: (a) to help the coachee understand and clearly express their own reasons and intrinsic motivations for change, (b) to support the coachee in formulating an action plan for achieving the change, and (c) to strengthen their commitment to the action plan.

It might also be useful to help the coachee fill out a **decisional balance sheet**. It includes the answers to the following four questions:[7]

- What are the benefits of your current behavior/activity?
- What are the costs of your current behavior/activity?
- What are the benefits of change?
- What are the costs of change?

Through answering these questions, the coachee should gain a better understanding about whether (and if yes, how much) the benefits of change outweigh its costs.

Recognizing that the balance is clearly in favor of the change can contribute to further strengthening a coachee's motivation to change.

COACHING QUESTIONS

COACHING QUESTIONS FOR MOTIVATIONAL INTERVIEWING

Questions for the 'Focusing' process:

- "What do you want to change?"
- "What should be different in the future?"
- "Where do you see a discrepancy between your current behavior and your goals?"
- "What are your real goals for the change?"

Questions for the 'Evoking' process:

- "Why do you want to change?"
- "Why is this change important for you?"
- "What is your main reason for the change?"
- "Tell me your three best reasons for making the change."
- "How does that behavior relate to your values?"
- "How do you feel about changing this behavior?"

Questions for the 'Planning' process:

- "What is your action plan for making the change happen?"
- "What exactly will you do?"
- "By when will you do this?"
- "Which concrete steps are you taking to ensure that you will succeed with the change?"
- "What would be the best next step?"
- "How confident are you that you will be able to make this change?"
- "On a scale of 1–10, what is your commitment to taking this step?"
- "What would it take for you to increase your commitment to 9 or 10?"

Source: inspired by contents in Miller & Rollnick (2013) and Passmore (2021).

The transtheoretical model

The MI approach is also in line with one of the most influential models of behavior change: the **transtheoretical model**.

This model predicts that people change their behaviors by gradually moving through the following **five stages** (see Figure 12):[8]

1. **Precontemplation.** The person is not ready for the change—they do not see a problem yet.
2. **Contemplation.** The person is getting ready for the change—they recognize that their current behavior could be problematic and start thinking about potential benefits and costs of changing.
3. **Preparation.** The person is ready for the change—they plan concrete action steps to make it happen.

4. **Action**. The person actually does things differently—they change their behavior.
5. **Maintenance**. The person sustains the new 'healthy' behavior—they successfully avoid relapsing to their old 'unhealthy' behavior.

MI can be particularly useful for encouraging coachees to progress from the *precontemplation* to the *contemplation* stage, and to support them during their *preparation* stage.

Other coaching strategies can be applied in the different stages of change, too:

- Awareness raising in the *precontemplation* stage (e.g. with the help of 360-degree-feedback, objective performance data, or assessment tools)
- Goal setting (e.g. with a goal hierarchy framework) in the *preparation* stage (see the section on goal setting below)
- Holding regular reviews and reflections on how a coachee is making progress in the *action* and *maintenance* stages[9]

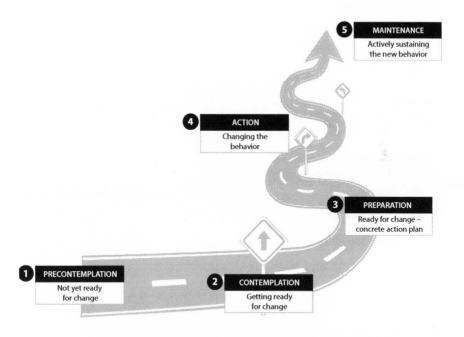

Figure 12 The five stages of the transtheoretical model [24]

COACHING BEST PRACTICE

WRITING A NEW STORY

One tool for helping coachees make a change is to ask them to 'write a new story.' Mandy Sinclair, a UK-based certified executive and life coach, explains two approaches in which this tool can be used:

"The first step is to write your current story and identify what you would like to change. Ask yourself questions such as: Am I choosing how I spend my time? Am I fulfilled? What do I love/hate doing? What do I like/dislike about myself? What do I think people like/dislike about me? How am I feeling on a day-to-day basis? Include both the 'being' and 'doing' areas of your life."

When coachees have identified specific elements of their current story they want to change, they can work together with their coach to find and commit to actions that will help them create a new story.

The second approach that Sinclair recommends to her coachees is to use free writing to imagine their future ideal life, maybe in 10 or even more years in the future:

"Make sure you have plenty of paper; take a pen in your hand and start writing. Just let the words flow. Don't correct any spelling, grammar, punctuation or worry about neatness or format. Keep writing until you have nothing else to say. If you really relax and let this happen it can be really eye-opening."

The 'new story' can then be used as a starting point for setting and actively pursuing goals that will bring the coachee nearer to their ideal future life. "I believe this second approach allows for true transformational change," says Sinclair.

Source: https://www.mebestlife.co.uk/lifecoaching/what-is-your-new-story/ (accessed 15 January 2021). With kind permission of Mandy Sinclair.

Typically, **ineffective behavior** (also known as 'bad habits') evolves as follows: a certain cue in a situation more or less automatically triggers a (negative) thought, which in turn leads to certain ineffective behaviors.

Let us take the following simple example: You are working on an important task when your cell phone notifies you about a new comment on your social media post (that's the cue). You immediately think "Oh, this could be interesting!" You interrupt your work to check your social media account. This is an ineffective behavior as it distracts you from your really important work.

What is needed in the *preparation* stage in this case is a '**cue-based action plan**.'[10] The coachees first need to recognize the cue. Then they can use the cue-based action plan that they have discussed with their coach to help them react to the cue in a more productive way.

Returning to the example above, a cue-based action plan in this situation could be to think about chocolate instead of grabbing your cell phone every time you get a new notification, and then rewarding yourself with a chocolate bar if you manage not to look at the cell phone until you finish your important task. Of course, an even better plan would be to get rid of the cue altogether (just switch off the notification function of your phone during periods of intense work).

Sustainable change, however, usually needs more than just applying a 'technique' that helps coachees progress from one stage to another. It is equally important for the coachee to understand 'what their heart says'—to explore their deep motivators, not only related to their work, but also to who they actually want to be.[11]

Goal setting and the hierarchy of goals

As we discussed in Chapter 2, goal setting is a crucial activity at the beginning of every coaching conversation. In essence, coaching conversations are goal-oriented conversations. Helping the coachee clearly understand and voice their goals is a key task of a coach.

We can distinguish between different **types of goals**:[12]

- **Distal goals and proximal goals**. Distal goals are long-term 'end goals' that describe an ideal future state which motivates and inspires the coachee (e.g. *"To create my own successful book publishing company"*). Proximal goals are shorter-term 'milestones' that form the basis for action planning (e.g. *"To convince the first author to be published by my new book publishing company"*).

- **Outcome goals, approach goals, and avoidance goals**. Outcome goals describe specific outcomes that a coachee wants to achieve (e.g. *"To have my thesis finished by the end of April"*). Approach goals are more oriented toward thinking about or doing something in a particular way (e.g. *"To take a more structured approach to decision making"*). Avoidance goals are about trying to abandon certain ineffective behaviors (e.g. *"To avoid being a complainer"*).
- **Performance and learning goals**. Performance goals describe how a coachee wants to perform specific tasks (e.g. *"To hold a presentation in a way that really engages the audience"*). When they set learning (or developmental) goals instead, coachees focus their attention "on the learning associated with task mastery, rather than on the performance of the task itself"[13] (e.g. *"To learn how to better connect to the audience during a presentation"*).
- **Complementary and conflicting goals**. Complementary goals support one another—if you reach one goal, this has a positive effect on the other goal, too. Conflicting goals, on the other hand, involve a trade-off: getting closer to one goal would bring you further away from achieving the other goal. The coach's task is to help the coachee identify potentially conflicting goals or find more complementary goals.
- **Goals that represent the coachee's own interests and goals that represent the interests of others**. To assess goal alignment, a coach might ask: Are the goals in line with the coachee's values and needs? Or are there discrepancies between the goals that others want the coachee to follow and what the coachee wants for themselves?

Gaining clarity about the type of goals that a coachee wants to follow is highly important for the coach. It is the basis for being able to support the coachee in identifying the right actions that will allow them to achieve their goals.

Coaches can use a **goal hierarchy framework** (see Figure 13) to get a better understanding of their coachees' goals and to spot potential conflicts between goals. The lower-order goals in the hierarchy are more specific and usually more behavior-oriented. They are instrumental for reaching the higher-order 'end goals,' which are more connected to the coachee's 'self' and their personal identity.[14]

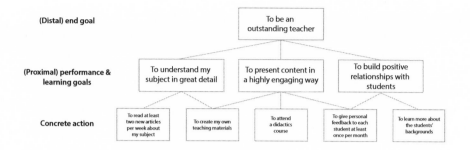

Figure 13 An example of a goal hierarchy framework[25]

YOUR OWN GOAL HIERARCHY FRAMEWORK

Develop your own goal hierarchy framework for a goal that really matters to you.

Step 1: Think about one really big goal (a distal 'end goal' that you would like to achieve within the next five years. Formulate the goal in a way that is connected to your personal identity ("I want to be …").

Step 2: Identify 3–5 more proximate performance and learning goals that are instrumental for reaching your end goal. Which tasks do you need to perform in order to achieve your big goal? What do you need to learn to make it happen?

Step 3: Think about concrete actions that could bring you closer to achieving your performance and learning goals. What are the next steps that you can take from tomorrow onward?

Create a diagram similar to the one in Figure 13 to visualize your goal hierarchy.

Through developing such a goal hierarchy framework for themselves with the help of the coach, coachees will get the chance to reflect on whether they are following the right (sub-)goals and give enough attention to the really important goals.

COACHING BEST PRACTICE

THE 'PERFECT DAY' EXERCISE

Regan Walsh is a certified executive coach and life coach based in Columbus, Ohio. "The goal of my coaching is to help you discover what livens your spirit," she says to her clients, "and then take purposeful and measurable steps to live that out."

One tool that she uses with her coachees to help them clarify their distal goals is the 'Perfect Day' exercise. "I invite them to consider how they feel and then write down what it would take in one day to feel that way," she explains. She encourages them to clearly visualize the day without any self-imposed limits. "What is the environment? When do you wake up? Who are you interacting with? What are you doing?"

Regan and her coachees then explore that day together. They try to identify themes, examine what's realistic, and discuss how the coachee could get there and sustain it.

Source: https://reganwalsh.com/is-this-it-how-to-find-your-passion-and-renew-your-life/ (accessed 8 February 2021). With kind permission of Regan Walsh.

It is easier for coachees to reach goals **over which they have some influence**. The coach could, for example, ask questions like *"How much influence do you have in achieving this goal?"* or *"What can you personally do to achieve this goal?"* to probe whether goals are really actionable. If the coachee thinks that reaching a particular goal is completely outside of their control, it might make sense to reformulate the goal.

Research has shown that people only set or accept challenging goals when they have a high level of **self-efficacy**: a feeling that they will be able to effectively execute the actions that are necessary to achieve their goals.[15]

One approach that coaches can use to help a coachee build self-efficacy is to **'ramp up' goals**, starting with those that are easier to reach first.[16] This can create confidence and motivation for tackling more challenging goals.

Assessing the **potentially negative consequences** of reaching a certain goal (e.g. *"Would reaching this goal potentially affect something else that you care about?"*) can help the coachee to see the whole picture.[17]

Another important factor in goal setting is to formulate goals in a way that makes it possible to obtain **feedback** on the degree of goal achievement during the goal implementation process.[18] Feedback is highly important for the coachee. It enables them to assess whether they are still 'on track' with implementing their goals. Feedback can also be a source of motivation for the coachee in sustaining goal-oriented action.

Before a coachee agrees to set a goal for themselves, a coach can check their level of **commitment to the goal** (e.g. by simply asking *"On a scale of 1–10, how committed are you to this goal?"*).

When there is a lack of commitment, it might make sense to reframe the goal.

Reframing a goal or problem

Coachees often expect their coach to help them **solve a problem**. A common procedure is to explore the problem situation together before developing options for solutions.

Coaches need to consider, however, that it is possible that the first framing of the problem might not be the one that leads to the best solution. How a problem is formulated (or 'framed') generally limits the number of solutions. Coaches can use reframing techniques to overcome these restrictions.

'Reframing' is a term that is used for changing our point of view on a problem situation. It is about reformulating the problem in a way that opens up the space for new (and potentially better) solutions.

Let us assume that you have the following problem: *"How can I stop my two little daughters from fighting every morning?"* You tried to make your expectations clear, you taught them how to channel their anger differently, you punished, you rewarded—but nothing worked. Maybe it is time to reframe the problem. You could, for example, ask *"How can I ensure that my two little daughters are less tired in the morning?"* You will soon come up with different options, such as sending them to bed earlier or giving them some orange juice when they wake up to raise their blood sugar levels. That might help you to eventually solve the problem.[19]

Reframing can be a powerful tool to ensure that the coach and coachee do not waste time working on the wrong problems.

Here are some strategies that coaches can use to help coachees reframe their problems:[20]

- **Missing factors.** Think about whether some contextual factors are missing in the current framing of the problem (e.g. are there any hidden influences on the situation, any prior events that you might have missed, or people who have not yet been considered?).
- **The right goal.** Is the coachee really pursuing the right goal? Is there a different proximate goal that might also help the coachee reach their higher-level end goal?
- **From victim to pilot.** Problems sometimes appear to be impossible to solve because of factors that are seemingly beyond the coachee's influence (e.g. the boss's inability to decide or unavailable resources). In this case, the coach could explore whether the problem can be reframed in a way that the coachee can actually do something about it.
- **The coachee's role in creating the problem.** The coach could help the coachee 'look in the mirror' and explore their own role in contributing to the problem.
- **Get an outside view.** It might be an eye-opener for the coachee to ask others how they see the problem situation.

In addition, **perspective-taking** can be particularly useful for problem situations that involve interpersonal issues. Listing other parties who are involved in the problem and deliberately trying to understand their needs, emotions, goals, context or point of view can help the coachee avoid making premature or wrong judgments about other people's actions.[21]

Reframing can help the coachee identify the right problem to solve. Changing the problem can often be more effective than getting stuck with suboptimal answers to the wrong question, or without any feasible solution at all.

COACHING QUESTIONS FOR REFRAMING A PROBLEM

General questions for reframing a problem:

- "Are we really solving the right problem?"
- "Do you think that we are focusing on the right things here?"
- "Did you learn something new about the problem since we met last time? Should we maybe reformulate the problem?"
- "What happened before the situation appeared? Did something like this happen in prior situations?"
- "Are we maybe missing something here about the problem situation?"
- "Which other people could have an influence on this situation?"
- "Which other short-term goal could you pursue in order to reach your end goal?"
- "Could there be a different explanation for what is going on?"
- "Which of your own actions have contributed to this situation?"
- "What is your own role in creating this situation?"
- "Whom could you ask to provide you with an outside view on the issue?"

Questions for perspective-taking:

- "Who else is involved in this situation?"
- "How does/might [person X] see the situation differently?"
- "How would you describe the problem from the other person's point of view?"
- "How might they feel about it and why?"
- "What might they want to achieve?"
- "Could there be a simple and 'innocent' explanation for their behavior?"
- "Which contextual factors could have an influence on their behavior?"
- "What could be the reasons for their behavior if we assume that they actually have good intentions?"
- "How could the problem be reframed if you both needed to agree on the problem formulation?"

Source: inspired by contents in Wedell-Wedellsborg (2020).

The action memo

An action memo (also known as a **task assignment record**)[22] is a simple tool for helping coachees to remain focused on their goal and on the agreed action steps between coaching sessions (see Figure 14).

It is basically a form on which the coachee provides answers to the following questions:[23]

- **Which task(s) will I complete** before the next coaching session? (e.g. *"I will write at least half a page every morning before I open my emails."*)
- What is the **purpose behind the task(s)**? (e.g. *"I want to overcome my tendency to procrastinate instead of writing."*)
- What are the **obstacles to completing the task**? (e.g. *"My email client automatically notifies me of incoming emails, which makes me want to take a quick look."*)
- What will I do to **overcome the obstacles**? (e.g. *"I will switch off the automatic notification in my email client."*)

At the beginning of the following coaching session, the action memo can then be used as a basis for a discussion about what the coachee implemented between the sessions and what they learned from it.

ACTION MEMO

Name _____

Date _____

Action	Due date	Purpose	Potential obstacles	How to overcome obstacles
I will write at least half a page every morning before I open my emails.	31.1.	I want to overcome my tendency to procrastinate instead of writing.	My email client automatically notifies me of incoming emails.	I will switch off the automatic notification function.
...	...	...	...	...

Figure 14 An example of an action memo[26]

COACHING TOOLS:
A BRIEF SUMMARY IN 10 POINTS

1. Coaches can use a range of different tools to **help coachees raise their self-awareness**. Examples include personality, values and strengths profiles, team roles tests, feedback from others, self-reflection exercises, and book reading assignments.

2. **Motivational interviewing** (MI) is a useful method for increasing a coachee's commitment to behavior change. When people speak about their motivation to change, this will raise the chance that they will succeed in actually changing their behaviors.

3. The **three phases of MI** are focusing (clarifying the change goals), evoking (voicing the motivation to change), and planning (committing to concrete action steps).

4. A **decisional balance sheet** (which weighs the benefits and cost of changing versus not changing) can be used to help a coachee recognize the benefits of behavior change.

5. The **transtheoretical model** explains the main stages that people usually go through when they change their behaviors (precontemplation, contemplation, preparation, action, maintenance).

6. Understanding **different types of goals** (distal end goals and proximal goals; outcome, approach, and avoidance goals; performance and learning goals; complementary and conflicting goals; own goals and the goals of others) can help a coachee gain more clarity about what they actually want to achieve.

7. A **goal hierarchy framework** can be used to help a coachee identify performance and learning goals that are instrumental for reaching their end goals.

8. **Reframing a goal or problem** can be an effective approach to opening up the space for new (and potentially better) solutions.

9. **Reframing strategies** include thinking about whether some contextual factors are missing in the current framing, challenging the current goal, leaving the 'victim mode,' exploring the coachee's own role in contributing to a situation, getting an outside view, and perspective-taking.

10. The **action memo** is a tool for keeping a coachee focused on goal-oriented action between coaching sessions.

Notes for Chapter 5

1   Athanasopoulou & Dopson (2018).
2   Kauffman & Coutu (2008).
3   Passmore (2021).
4   Miller & Rollnick (2013).
5   Miller & Rollnick (2013).
6   Miller & Rollnick (2013).
7   Passmore (2021).
8   Prochaska & DiClemente (1982; 2005); Grant (2021).
9   Grant (2021); Passmore (2021).
10 Natale & Diamante (2005), p. 370.
11 Gray (2006).
12 Grant (2021).
13 Grant (2021), p. 122.
14 Gregory et al. (2011).
15 Gregory et al. (2011).
16 Gregory et al. (2011).
17 Starr (2016).
18 Grant (2021).
19 Bregman (2015).
20 Wedell-Wedellsborg (2020).
21 Wedell-Wedellsborg (2020).
22 Neenan (2008).
23 Neenan (2008).
24 Graphic representation by the author based on contents in Prochaska & DiClemente (1982; 2005) and Grant (2021); source of road illustration: pixabay.com.
25 Source: author, inspired by Grant (2021), p. 126.
26 Source: graphical representation by the author, inspired by concepts in Neenan (2008).

A CONCLUDING NOTE

Congratulations on getting this far! By now you've hopefully learned a lot about the key principles and tools of professional coaching.

I hope that you will be able to use the ideas, methods, and coaching questions from this book to enhance your own coaching skills.

Even if you are not thinking about becoming a professional coach, you can use these principles and tools to help other people develop and make progress on whatever they aspire to do or be.

When you apply the principles of coaching, you will be able to:

- **ask better questions,**
- **listen more carefully**, and
- **hold deeper conversations** focused on the needs and goals of people you care for.

This will not only make you a valued coach, but also a person who **makes a difference in other people's lives**.

If you think that this book has made a contribution to your own learning and could also be of benefit to your team members, colleagues, students, or friends, **please share it** with them, too.

As an independent publisher and author with a mission to create concise, approachable, and affordable textbooks that can make a difference to a wider audience, I would be particularly grateful if you could help to spread the word about this book through **writing an honest online review**. It takes just a few minutes to write two or three lines, but it could have a big positive impact!

The more people who adopt a coaching mindset and develop coaching skills, the more we can help others unlock their potential.

So LET'S START COACHING—and let us feel the joy of helping others grow and thrive!

Bibliography

Ackerman, C. E. (2020). 25 CBT techniques and worksheets for cognitive behavioral therapy. https://positivepsychology.com/cbt-cognitive-behavioral-therapy-techniques-worksheets/, published 16 October 2020, accessed 30 December 2020.

Athanasopoulou, A., & Dopson, S. (2018). A systematic review of executive coaching outcomes: Is it the journey or the destination that matters the most? *The Leadership Quarterly, 29*(1), 70–88.

Bachkirova, T., Arthur, L., & Reading, E. (2021). Evaluating a coaching and mentoring program: Challenges and solutions. In: Passmore, J., & Tee, D. (eds), *Coaching Researched: A Coaching Psychology Reader*, pp. 361–378. Hoboken, NJ: Wiley.

Belton, S. (2020). *Change Your Life in 5: Practical Steps to Making Meaningful Changes in Your Life*. London: Eddison Books.

Bono, J. E., Purvanova, R. K., Towler, A. J., & Peterson, D. B. (2009). A survey of executive coaching practices. *Personnel Psychology, 62*(2), 361–404.

Bregman, P. (2015). Are you trying to solve the wrong problem? https://hbr.org/2015/12/are-you-solving-the-wrong-problem, published 7 December 2015, accessed 4 March 2021.

Britton, J. J. (2015). Expanding the coaching conversation: Group and team coaching. *Industrial and Commercial Training, 47*(3), 116–120.

Bungay Stanier, M. (2016). *The Coaching Habit: Say Less, Ask More & Change the Way You Lead Forever*. Toronto, ON: Box of Crayons Press.

Burt, D., & Talati, Z. (2017). The unsolved value of executive coaching: A meta-analysis of outcomes using randomised control trial studies. *International Journal of Evidence Based Coaching and Mentoring, 15*(2), 17.

Cardon, A. (2008). Powerful coaching questions. https://www.metasysteme-coaching.eu/english/-powerful-coaching-questions/, published 2008, accessed 7 December 2020.

Cherniss, C., Extein, M., Goleman, D., & Weissberg, R. P. (2006). Emotional intelligence: what does the research really indicate? *Educational Psychologist, 41*(4), 239–245.

Cox, E. & Bachkirova, T. (2021). Coaching with emotion: How coaches deal with difficult emotional situations. In: Passmore, J., & Tee, D. (eds), *Coaching Researched: A Coaching Psychology Reader*, pp. 167–182. Hoboken, NJ: Wiley.

de Haan, E., Bertie, C., Day, A., & Sills, C. (2010). Clients' critical moments of coaching: Toward a "client model" of executive coaching. *Academy of Management Learning & Education, 9*(4), 607–621.

Dimas, I. D., Rebelo, T., & Lourenço, P. R. (2016). Team coaching: One more clue for fostering team effectiveness. *European Review of Applied Psychology, 66*(5), 233–242.

Ellis, A. (1994). *Reason and Emotion in Psychotherapy*. Secausus, NJ: Birch Lane Press.

Evers, W. J., Brouwers, A., & Tomic, W. (2006). A quasi-experimental study on management coaching effectiveness. *Consulting Psychology Journal: Practice and Research, 58*(3), 174–182.

Feldman, D. C., & Lankau, M. J. (2005). Executive coaching: A review and agenda for future research. *Journal of Managment, 31*(6), 829–848.

Fillery-Travis, A. & Lane, D. A. (2021). Does coaching work or are we asking the wrong question? In: Passmore, J., & Tee, D. (eds), *Coaching Researched: A Coaching Psychology Reader*, pp. 47–64. Hoboken, NJ: Wiley.

Forbes Coaches Council (2018). 16 powerful questions coaches ask their clients to help achieve their goals. https://www.forbes.com/sites/forbescoachescouncil/2018/06/21/16-powerful-questions-coaches-ask-their-clients-to-help-achieve-their-goals/?sh=44d974765e0c, published 21 June 2018, accessed 7 December 2020.

Garvin, D. A. (2013). How Google sold its engineers on management. *Harvard Business Review, 91*(12), 74–82.

Gates, B. (2013). Teachers need real feedback. https://www.ted.com/talks/bill_gates_teachers_need_real_feedback#t-2483, accessed 30 October 2020.

Good, D., Yeganeh, B., & Yeganeh, R. (2013). Cognitive behavioral executive coaching. *Research in Organizational Change and Development, 21*, 175–200.

Grant, A. M. (2003). The impact of life coaching on goal attainment, metacognition and mental health. *Social Behavior and Personality: An International Journal, 31*(3), 253–263.

Grant, A. (2021). An integrated model of goal-focused coaching: An evidence-based framework for teaching and practice. In: Passmore, J., & Tee, D. (eds), *Coaching Researched: A Coaching Psychology Reader*, pp. 115–140. Hoboken, NJ: Wiley.

Gregory, J. B., Beck, J. W., & Carr, A. E. (2011). Goals, feedback, and self-regulation: Control theory as a natural framework for executive coaching. *Consulting Psychology Journal: Practice and Research, 63*(1), 26.

Gollwitzer, P. M. (1996). The volitional benefits of planning. In: Gollwitzer P. M., & Bargh, J. A. (eds), *The Psychology of Action: Linking Cognition and Motivation to Behavior*, pp. 287–312. New York, NY: Guilford Press.

Grant, A. M. (2017). Solution-focused cognitive–behavioral coaching for sustainable high performance and circumventing stress, fatigue, and burnout. *Consulting Psychology Journal: Practice and Research, 69*(2), 98.

Grant, A., & O'Connor, S. (2019). A brief primer for those new to coaching research and evidence-based practice. *The Coaching Psychologist, 15*(1), 3–10.

Gray, D. E. (2006). Executive coaching: Towards a dynamic alliance of psychotherapy and transformative learning processes. *Management Learning, 37*(4), 475–497.

Green, S., Grant, A. M., & Rynsaardt, J. (2007). Evidence-based life coaching for senior high school students: Building hardiness and hope. *International Coaching Psychology Review, 2*(1), 24–32.

Hawkins, P. (2009). Coaching supervision. In: Cox, E., Bachkirova, T., & Clutterbuck, D. (eds), *The Complete Handbook of Coaching*, 2nd ed., pp. 391–404. London: Sage.

Hawkins, P & Smith N. (2013). *Coaching, Mentoring and Organizational Consultancy: Supervision and Development*. 2nd ed. Maidenhead: McGraw-Hill/Open University Press.

Ibarra, H., & Scoular, A. (2019). The leader as coach. *Harvard Business Review, 97*(6), 110–119.

Joo, B. K. (2005). Executive coaching: A conceptual framework from an integrative review of practice and research. *Human Resource Development Review, 4*(4), 462–488.

Kauffman, C. & Coutu, D. (2008). The realities of executive coaching. *Harvard Business Review Research Report* (Boston, MA: Harvard Business School Publishing), 1–32.

Lai, Y.-L. & Palmer, S. (2019). Psychology in executive coaching: An integrated literature review. *Journal of Work-Applied Management, 11*(2), 143–164.

Lane, D. A. & Corrie, S. (2021). Does coaching psychology need the concept of formulation? In: Passmore, J., & Tee, D. (eds), *Coaching Researched: A Coaching Psychology Reader*, pp. 97–114. Hoboken, NJ: Wiley.

Locke, E. A. (1996). Motivation through conscious goal setting. *Applied and Preventive Psychology, 5*(2), 117–124.

Loehr, A. (2008). Five tips for effective coaching questions. https://www.anneloehr.com/2008/12/29/five-tips-for-effective-coaching-questions/, accessed 4 February 2021.

McCauley, C. D., & Hezlett, S. A. (2001). Individual development in the workplace. In: Anderson, N., Ones, D., Sinangil H. K. & Viswesvaran, C. (eds), *Handbook of Industrial, Work, and Organizational Psychology*, Vol. 2, pp. 313–335. London: Sage.

Miller, W. R., & Rollnik, S. (2013). *Motivational Interviewing: Helping People Change*. 3rd ed. New York, NY: The Guilford Press.

Natale, S. M., & Diamante, T. (2005). The five stages of executive coaching: Better process makes better practice. *Journal of Business Ethics, 59*(4), 361–374.

Neenan, M. (2008). From cognitive behaviour therapy (CBT) to cognitive behaviour coaching (CBC). *Journal of Rational-Emotive & Cognitive-Behavior Therapy, 26*(1), 3–15.

O'Connor, J., & Lages, A. (2019). *Coaching the Brain: Practical Applications of Neuroscience of Coaching*. London: Routledge.

Open University (2016). Summarising and reflecting. https://www.open.edu/openlearn/ money-business/leadership-management/three-principles-coaching-approach/content-section-3, accessed 12 January 2021.

Passmore, J. (2021). Addressing deficit performance through coaching: Using motivational interviewing for performance improvement at work. In: Passmore, J., & Tee, D. (eds), *Coaching Researched: A Coaching Psychology Reader*, pp. 83–96. Hoboken, NJ: Wiley.

Passmore, J., & Fillery-Travis, A. (2011). A critical review of executive coaching research: A decade of progress and what's to come. *Coaching: An International Journal of Theory, Research and Practice, 4*(2), 70–88.

Passmore, J., & Tee, D. (eds) (2021). *Coaching Researched: A Coaching Psychology Reader*. Hoboken, NJ: Wiley.

Peterson, D. B. (2006). People are complex and the world is messy: A behavior-based approach to executive coaching. In: Stober, D. R. & Grant, A. M. (eds), *Evidence-based Coaching Handbook: Putting Best Practices to Work for Your Clients*, pp. 51–76. Hoboken, NJ: Wiley.

Peterson, D. B. (2011). Executive coaching: A critical review and recommendations for advancing the practice. In: Zedeck, S. (ed), *APA Handbook of Industrial and Organizational Psychology*, Vol. 2, pp. 527–566. Washington, DC: American Psychological Association.

Prochaska, J. O., & DiClemente, C. C. (1982). Transtheoretical therapy: toward a more integrative model of change. *Psychotherapy: Theory, Research & Practice, 19*(3), 276–288.

Prochaska, J. O., & DiClemente, C. C. (2005). The transtheoretical approach. In: Norcross, J. C., & Goldfield, M. R. (eds), *Handbook of Psychotherapy Integration*, 2nd ed., pp. 147–171. Oxford: Oxford University Press.

Rekalde, I., Landeta, J., Albizu, E., & Fernandez-Ferrin, P. (2017). Is executive coaching more effective than other management training and development methods? *Management Decision, 55*(10), 2149–2162.

Schmidt, E., Rosenberg, J., & Eagle, A. (2019). *Trillion Dollar Coach: The Leadership Handbook of Silicon Valley's Bill Campbell*. New York, NY: HarperCollins.

Scoular, P. A. (2009). How do you pick a coach? *Harvard Business Review, 87*(1), 96.

Sherman, S. & Freas, A. (2004). The wild west of executive coaching. *Harvard Business Review, 82*(11), 82–90.

Six, F. (2005). *The Trouble With Trust: The Dynamics of Interpersonal Trust Building*. Cheltenham, UK: Edward Elgar.

Six, F., Nooteboom, B., & Hoogendoorn, A. (2010). Actions that build interpersonal trust: A relational signalling perspective. *Review of Social Economy, 68*(3), 285–315.

Starr, J. (2016). *The Coaching Manual*. 4th ed. Harlow: Pearson.

Sternad, D. (2020). *Effective Management: Developing Yourself, Others and Organizations*. London: Macmillan International Higher Education/Red Globe Press.

Stewart, L. J., Palmer, S., Wilkin, H., & Kerrin, M. (2021). Toward a model of coaching transfer: Operationalizing coaching success and facilitators and barriers to transfer. In: Passmore, J., & Tee, D. (eds), *Coaching Researched: A Coaching Psychology Reader*, pp. 361–378. Hoboken, NJ: Wiley.

Stoltzfus, T. (2008). *Coaching Questions: A Coach's Guide to Powerful Asking Skills*. Virginia Beach, VA: Tony Stoltzfus.

Sue-Chan, C., & Latham, G. P. (2004). The relative effectiveness of external, peer, and self-coaches. *Applied Psychology, 53*(2), 260–278.

Su, A. J. (2014). The questions good coaches ask. https://hbr.org/2014/12/the-questions-good-coaches-ask, published 12 December 2014, accessed 7 December 2020.

Tkach, J. T. & DiGirolamo, J. A. (2021). The state and future of coaching supervision. In: Passmore, J., & Tee, D. (eds), *Coaching Researched: A Coaching Psychology Reader*, pp. 23–42. Hoboken, NJ: Wiley.

Vickers, A. & Bavister, S. (2010). *Confident Coaching: The Fundamental Theories and Concepts of Coaching*. London: Hodder Education.

Wasylyshyn, K. M. (2003). Executive coaching: An outcome study. *Consulting Psychology Journal: Practice and Research, 55*(2), 94–106.

Wedell-Wedellsborg, T. (2020). *What's Your Problem: To Solve Your Toughest Problems, Change the Problems You Solve*. Boston, MA: Harvard Business Review Press.

Weger Jr, H., Castle, G. R., & Emmett, M. C. (2010). Active listening in peer interviews: The influence of message paraphrasing on perceptions of listening skill. *The International Journal of Listening, 24*(1), 34–49.

Whitmore, Sir J. (2017). *Coaching for Performance: The Principles and Practice of Coaching and Leadership*. 5th ed. London/Boston: Nicholas Brealey Publishing.

Williams, H. & Palmer, S. (2018). CLARITY: A case study application of a cognitive behavioural coaching model. *European Journal of Applied Positive Psychology, 2*, article 6, 1–12.

Index

A

AAA exercise 83
ABCDE model 41-42, 47-48
ABCDE model (exercise) 47
ABC model 41
accountability 19, 37, 60-61
accountability email 62
accreditation bodies 17
action memo 38, 102-103
action plan 12, 14, 22, 40
active listening 69, 75-77, 85
advice 8, 9, 22
Allen, Melanie 46
anxieties 33
assessment phase 57, 66
awareness of others 81, 85
awareness *see self-awareness*

B

behavior change 10, 90-95
Belton, Sue 83

C

Campbell, Bill 20
career counseling 8, 24
certification institutions 17
change process 90 *see also behavior change*
CLEAR framework 40
coachability 21
coach (definition) 6, 24
coaching conversation 18, 24, 27-28, 36, 60
coaching mindset 69, 70-71, 85
coaching outcomes *see outcomes of coaching*
coaching process 51-52, 66

coaching questions *see effective coaching questions*
coaching questions (boxes) 31, 33, 35, 38, 44, 61, 91, 101
coaching session 28, 48, 51, 59-60, 66
coaching supervision 17, 64
cognitive behavioral coaching (CBC) 40, 42, 43, 44, 48
cognitive behavioral theory (CBT) 40, 41, 42
collaborative attitude 22, 70
commitment to a goal 98
confidentiality 21, 57
conflicting goals 96
conflicts 18, 20
constructive feedback 78, 80 *see also feedback*
consulting 9, 24
contract 55
conversational techniques 18
counseling 8, 24
cue-based action plan 95

D

daily journal 61
decisional balance sheet 91, 103
decision making 36
de Jong, Kris 14
deliberative mindset 36
Discovery Questionnaire 58-59
distal goals 95
duration of coaching assignments 18

E

effective coaching 10, 21, 24
effective coaching questions 72-73
Ellis, Albert 41
emotional intelligence 69

P

Page, Larry 20
performance goals 30, 31, 96
personal development 11-12
personality 14, 16, 58
personality profiles 88
personal mission statement 12-13
perspective-taking 100-101
Peterson, David B. 12
prioritizing 36
problem solving 10, 98, 100
progress review 51, 60-61, 64, 66
psychologist 16
psychotherapy 8, 24, 90
purpose in life 12
purpose of coaching 6, 51-54, 66

Q

quality of life 13
questioning approach 6, 7, 69
questioning skills 72
questions *see also coaching questions
     (boxes)*
     solution-oriented 74-75

R

reality
     external *see external reality*
     internal *see internal reality*
Reality (phase in the GROW model)
     32
reflection 10, 63-64, 66
reflective diary 65
reframing (a goal or a problem) 98, 99,
     100, 101, 103
relationship between the coach and
     coachee 19, 21, 51, 56, 66
relationship with the organization 55
removing obstacles *see obstacles*
return on investment 10

S

Schlafman, Steve 58
Schmidt, Eric 20
Scoular, Anne 15, 28
self-assessment 12
self-awareness 5, 6, 10, 32, 78, 79, 87,
     103
self-confidence 10
self-efficacy 10, 22, 98
self-reflection exercises 88
Sherman, Stratford 33
Sinclair, Mandy 94
SMART goals 30
Socrates 7
Socratic method 7
sponsoring organization 16, 55
stakeholders 53, 58
strengths 10, 12, 20, 58, 88
strengths profiles 88
summarizing 19, 77, 85
supervision *see coaching supervision*

T

task assignment record, *see action
     memo*
teaching 9, 22
team 11, 18, 19-21
team coaching 19, 20, 21, 24
team performance 11
team roles tests 88
TED model 72
training 12
transition 18
transparency 21
transtheoretical model 87, 92, 93, 103
trust 20, 21, 57, 66
trust-building actions 57
types of goals 30, 95, 96, 103

V

values 14, 20, 96
victim mindset 82
videos 3
vision board 12

W

well-being 10, 13
Wheel of Life 12
Whitmore, Sir John 29, 76, 78
Will (phase in the GROW model) 36
work-life balance 11
work performance 10
work-related attitudes 10

Dr. Dietmar Sternad is a management professor who teaches the Coaching Skills Program as part of the International Business Management master's program at Carinthia University of Applied Sciences (Austria). He is an alumnus of the GLOCOLL (Harvard Business School) and IMTA (CEE-MAN) management teacher development programs and won several national and international awards for teaching excellence and for the development of learning materials (e.g. from the *Academy of Management*, *Emerald Publishing*, and *Oikos*). Dietmar also has years of experience as an executive in book publishing and media companies, and in consulting, training, and coaching top managers and high potentials. He is author of several internationally acclaimed textbooks, such as *Effective Management: Developing Yourself, Others and Organizations* (London, Macmillan International Higher Education).

Apply the strategies and tools of smart problem solving—and succeed in work and life!

What do Albert Einstein, Elon Musk, Sherlock Holmes, and Mahatma
Gandhi's six-year old granddaughter have in common?
They are all masters of **the art of smart problem solving**—
a highly sought-after skill that you can learn, too!

Available wherever good books and ebooks are sold.

Essential reading for coaches of international teams

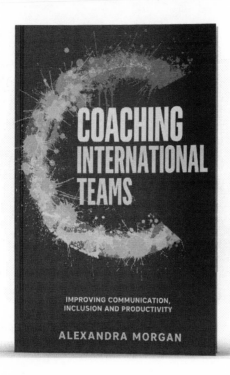

This easily accessible book guides you through key (and often hidden)
reasons for communication breakdown in international teams.
As a coach or leader of an international team, you will be
able to improve understanding and intercultural awareness,
and see productivity and collaboration improve as a result.

From February 2022 on
available wherever good books and ebooks are sold.

econcise
Concise books for smart learners

Made in the USA
Las Vegas, NV
07 September 2023

76992439R00074